The Complete Dales Walker

1. The Northern Dales

Geoffrey White

Dalesman Publishing Company Limited,
Stable Courtyard, Broughton Hall,
Skipton, North Yorkshire BD23 3AE

First Published 1994
Reprinted 1996

Text © exors Geoffrey White
Maps © Ken Johnston

Cover: Aysgarth Falls by Deryck Hallam

Typeset by Lands Services
Printed by Hubbard Print

A British Library Cataloguing in Publication
record is available for this book

ISBN 1 85568 070 X

Every effort has been made to ensure that information given on
walks is accurate and up to date. Readers must seek permission
where necessary to use footpaths and refer to the appropriate
up-to-date Ordnance Survey maps for more detailed guidance.
Details of recent footpath diversions can usually be obtained from
National Park and tourist information centres.

CONTENTS

INTRODUCTION 5

LOWER WENSLEYDALE 7
Walk 1   Ripon and Fountains Abbey 9
Walk 2   Sawley, Picking Gill and Eavestone Lake 12
Walk 3   Grantley and Lumley Moor 15
Walk 4   Dallowgill 18
Walk 5   Grewelthorpe and Hackfall 21
Walk 6   Ilton Temple 24
Walk 7   Colsterdale and Witton Fell 26
Walk 8   Jervaulx Abbey and the River Ure 29

UPPER WENSLEYDALE 32
Walk 9   Great Haw 34
Walk 10   Penhill 37
Walk 11   Coverdale and Walden 39
Walk 12   Walden Beck and Buckden Pike 43
Walk 13   Bolton Castle and Apedale 47
Walk 14   Aysgarth Falls 50
Walk 15   Askrigg's Waterfalls 52
Walk 16   Wether Fell and Bardale 55
Walk 17   Semerwater and the Stake Pass 57
Walk 18   Hardraw and Great Shunner Fell 60
Walk 19   Hell Gill 63

SWALEDALE 66
Walk 20   Whitcliffe, Applegarth and Clapgate Gill 69
Walk 21   Marske Beck 73
Walk 22   Marrick Priory and Fremington Edge 76
Walk 23   Arkengarthdale and Slei Gill 79
Walk 24   Hard Level Gill and Great Pinseat 82
Walk 25   Whitaside Moor and Apedale Head 85
Walk 26   Gunnerside Gill 87
Walk 27   Ivelet Bridge and Oxnop Gill 90
Walk 28   Thwaite and Muker 93
Walk 29   Muker, River Swale, Keld and Kisdon Hill 95

Walk 30   Round Kisdon Hill   98
Walk 31   The Waterfalls of Keld 100
Walk 32   West Stonedale and Tan Hill 102
Walk 33   Wain Wath Force and Whitsundale 105
Walk 34   Nine Standards Rigg 107

INTRODUCTION

ALTHOUGH the Yorkshire Dales National Park becomes more popular year by year with both motorist and walker, even the most enthusiastic Dales lover cannot be expected to have an intimate knowledge of all the nooks and crannies in it. This book attempts to fill some of the gaps, but by no means all, as well as effecting an introduction to the newcomer. All the walks are circular and they vary in length. To those finding them not long enough may I suggest combining two adjoining walks – with perhaps a short motor ride between? Long distance walkers could no doubt devise their own connecting links or find some value in the list of recognised long walks in the appendix. If a walk ever departs from the right of way it will be clearly stated. Only on the high fells will this occur, and here there is a tradition of public access – a privilege not a right. On open moors and fells I have never been denied the privilege, but on rare occasions when shooting parties have been encountered I have given the guns a wide berth!

The northern dales of Wensleydale and Swaledale have everything to commend them: wild fell; outstanding views; extensive moorland; well-trodden tracks; places of historical and geographical interest; geological characteristics giving distinctive shapes to the hills and valleys; waterfalls of beauty and charm. Many books have been written about this delightful countryside, some being quoted in the appendix. I would commend *The Yorkshire Dales* by Marie Hartley and Joan Ingilby, famous authors who have lived in Askrigg for a great number of years and are as familiar with the Dales as any writer living. In reading their chapters on Swaledale, Wensleydale, Coverdale, Bishopdale and Walden a considerable contribution is made to the interest of the walks covered by this book.

The map for each walk is intended to be self-explanatory, but the reader is recommended to use in addition the Ordnance Survey 1:25,000 Outdoor Leisure Map of the Yorkshire Dales (Northern and Central) and also 1:50,000 Sheets 98 and 99 (Wensleydale & Wharfedale, and Ripon) for pleasure, interest and safety of the excursion.

What to wear: Strong footwear – my own preference is for walking boots for the support they give to the ankles, grip on the ground and resistance to bog; thick socks – some prefer two pairs – even three; warm clothing.

What to carry: Waterproof – preferably anorak or cagoule; this guide; O.S. map; compass – chiefly for interest but you may get lost in mist; rucksack; some food, even if it is your intention to return for a meal; a simple first aid kit.

If the weather turns bad, do not hesitate to return by the way you have come. Conditions in the Dales can change very quickly, cloud or snow storms altering the outlook in minutes.

Lower Wensleydale

Ripon and Lower Wensleydale

THE ancient city of Ripon is well worth an extended visit for its own sake, and there is much to explore and admire. Most important, of course, is the Cathedral together with the extensive Market Place and surrounding narrow streets and alleys. To explore a little further, there are riverside paths to find which make pleasant walks; such a walk would take one to Hewick Bridge and across to the village of Sharow and back to Ripon over North Bridge. The towpath of the canal takes one past the racecourse to join a riverside path along the Ure to look across the river to Newby Hall, and perhaps return via Bishop Monkton and Littlethorpe.

Those who may be interested in Ripon's history and development from the earliest times could do no better than procure and study the most excellent Dalesman book by the Ripon Civic Society entitled 'Ripon, Some Aspects of its History' published in 1972. Sufficient here to say that St. Wilfred's Minster Church was consecrated in 672 and, ever since, there has been a community in Ripon, administered by the clergy in the early days but later by the Aldermen whose chief was called the Wakeman (predecessor of the Mayor). He caused a horn to be blown every night at nine o'clock and kept watch thereafter for the prevention of crime in the town. This custom of hornblowing is still kept at 9 o'clock every evening.

Ripon is at the confluence of the Rivers Skell and Laver with the River Ure. Some very fine motor rides from Ripon include a particularly good one through Masham to Feasby and up Colsterdale beside the River Burn. Another short journey leads to the splendid Hackfall Woods at the heart of lower Wensleydale.

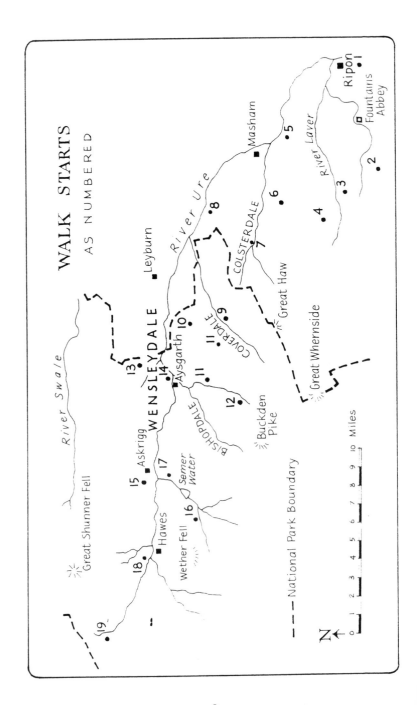

Ripon and Fountains Abbey

Ripon, in a stretch of rolling open country, is not in Wensleydale, but from the south and south-west it is the gateway to it. Fountains Abbey is one of Britain's most famous national monuments and now in the care of the National Trust. For years it was the overlord of the dales and so beautifully situated in upland country, makes the perfect objective for the first walk of this volume. Ripon itself is a small attractive market town on the River Ure, with a cathedral going back to the 15th century – the west front is particularly fine. It is a city of tradition, notably in the blowing of the Wakeman's horn at 9pm every evening at the Mayor's house and at the market cross.

WALKING out of Ripon on the Pateley Bridge road, about 300 yards beyond the bridge (round the first bend), there is a signpost on the left indicating the footpath to Studley Roger. Go over the stile by the side of it and take a faint track through the centre of the field, towards the church spire seen ahead. Pass through a small gate in a post and rail fence; go over a substantial stile over an electric fence; make towards the left-hand corner of the field, in line with the village which is now in sight; pass two gnarled trees; and go through a gate into a short lane leading to the village street – delightful, quiet and clean.

Cross the road and follow a sign pointing the way to Fountains Abbey. Go over a churned-up field to a stile over a barbed wire fence; pass through a clean pasture to a gate in the wall of Studley Royal Park; and continue on the track through the park, where deer abound, to reach the straight park road at a point opposite an ice house. This is below a small copse on the opposite hillside. Turn to the right on the road and at the cross roads look back for a grand view of Ripon cathedral beyond the end of the drive. Now turn down to the lake, following the sign to Fountains Abbey. Still on the park road, keep alongside the delightful lake which supports waterfowl and wild life, crossing a cattle grid to make for the gate house and restaurant. There is no admission on Christmas Eve, Christmas and Boxing Day.

From the gate, keep to the main drive, although one may wander at will. The route suggested here is one of many, but do not miss the abbey itself and the surprise view. Pass beautifully kept trees and water gardens in the Italian style, lovely lawns and landscaping conforming to the territory, and wildflowers in profusion from snowdrops onwards according to season. Rounding the bend, the noble ruin of the largest Cistercian abbey in Europe comes into

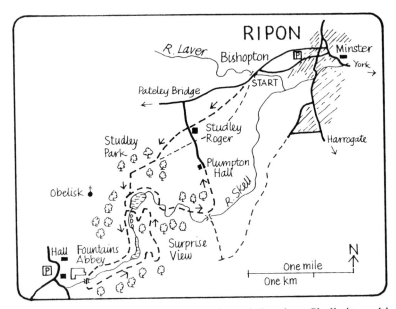

sight. Situated in the tree-lined valley of the river Skell, it could not be in a more beautiful setting.

After you have explored the abbey and perhaps the hall (built in the reign of James I) and the 12th century gate house, return to the east end of the ruin and cross to the other side of the valley on a track over the river. Turn sharply left to return on a wide track through trees, which soon comes down to the riverside where it is pleasant to wander by calm waters and weirs. At a sharp bend, where the water becomes a lake, look out for a white stone from which a track goes uphill to the right. Take it and, after it has swept around to the left near the top, you will see a summer-house. Here is the surprise view where you may take your fill of its beauty and regain your breath.

Continue along the top on a woodland trail, passing another summer-house on the left (or its foundations, for it was dismantled when last visited but, from appearances, was to be rebuilt). Occasional glimpses of the grounds below on the left and another lake on the right may be seen through the trees. On reaching another folly, go downhill on the left and through a tunnel just beyond it, emerging on the lawns of the water gardens. A palladian temple is on the left. Turn right, following the water, now in the form of a canal, to the weir which gushes on to the lake first seen earlier in the day. Here cross the substantial stepping stones back to the gate house and down to the lake shore, wandering to the lower end and passing over a footbridge.

Turn left and in the delectable little valley of the river Skell – now on your left – go downstream, crossing five stone footbridges. This valley is still in the deer park, but after crossing the fifth bridge the boundary wall is reached. Go through a gate in a high fence and immediately over a stile to continue down-valley through private woods on a track carrying a right of way, near the end of which you will see on your right a wooden footbridge over the river. This could lead to an alternative way back to Ripon, but for today's journey do not cross it. Keep straight on, on the left bank, on a track which soon bears away to the left through the wood, emerging on the left side of a field, across which are clear views of Ripon dominated by the minster. Beyond it, across the Plain of York, are the Hambleton Hills.

On a cart track, pass Plumpton Hall Farm, where the track becomes a tarmac road. Soon the gates to Studley Royal Park are reached. Pass through the village as far as the cross tracks which will be recognised. Turn right at the signpost for Ripon, and retrace your steps.

Sawley, Picking Gill
and Eavestone Lake

This is a most satisfying walk over pasture land, through three wood-lands, passing three lakes and giving good distant views. The lakes are artificial but their setting, especially at Eavestone, is delightful. If travelling from Ripon, take the B6256 road for five miles and, passing the entrance to Grantley Hall on the right, take the next immediate turn on the left to Sawley. There is adequate parking space on the edges of the village green.

WALK forward along the road for a short distance, passing the Sawley Arms Inn and the church, to reach a road junction sign-posted to Brimham Rocks and Pateley Bridge. Just across the road there is a wall stile by a Footpath signpost. From this stile aim towards a line of trees seen in front. Pass through the gateway at the right-hand side of the line of trees, and walk towards the power-line post in the middle of the field. The buildings of Lacon Hall will be seen ahead and this is the next objective; make straight for them until you reach an angle in a holly hedge. There is a fence stile a few paces to the left. Cross the field to Lacon Hall and turn right between buildings to a gate. Go across a small enclosure to the fence corner, and go over the low fence and across a shallow stream. Pass through a gap in the wall on your right, then climb the hill, following the wall side on your left. Where the wall turns away at an angle, continue upwards to the corner of the wood at the top of the hill. There is now a rough stone stile over a wall corner by a waymarked fence post. Cross the next field diagonally to reach another wood corner where there is a waymarked gate into a green lane (known as Green Lane). As you cross this field it is worth noting the remains of an ancient cross, Lacon Cross; standing at a high point, it is a good place at which to pause and admire the view.

Turn right along the lane for a short distance and pass through a gateway into a large field. Now head diagonally and down to a gate into Picking Gill Wood. The gate bears a large notice stating "Please properly close the gate". Descend through the wood to join a wide track in the valley. At this point it is worth turning right for a very short distance to see the lake in Picking Gill, but return to the same point, and continue for 70 yards and no further to a grass track on the right. Foliage may hide the entrance to this track in Summer. It leads almost immediately to a bridge of unusual structure, having no parapet and being entirely overgrown with

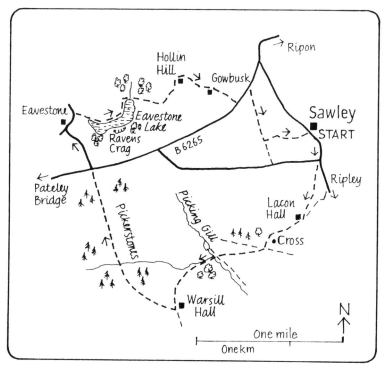

bracken and bluebells. The route is now upwards through the woods and becomes a sunken track leading to a gate at the edge of the wood.

Continue uphill across three fields towards Warsill Hall Farm. In the first make for a gateway to the left of a ruined building, then upwards along a line of trees. Cross the last field diagonally, with farm buildings over to the left, to cross a rough wall stile, which is some 25 yards to the right of a group of trees at the junction of tracks just above the farm. Now turn right on a clear farm track following the wall and hedge on the right, to cross a field with a wood over to the left. Then follow a stone wall on the right to reach a waymarked gate in the field corner leading into forestry.

The main forest track now goes straight for a little over half a mile, but on the way, note on the left a large forest hut. This is Pickerstones. There is a track behind the hut and then for a very short distance to the right, leading to another lake which is worth visiting. There are bird hides and the area is potentially interesting. Return to the hut and continue on the forest track. Emerging from the forest at a waymarked gate, follow the wall on the right to the main road, the B6265. Cross straight over into a minor gated road

13

leading to the village of Eavestone. Take the bend to the right and, shortly after a bend to the left, note a public footpath sign on the right into a wood. This is the entry to Eavestone Lake.

The path descends steeply through the wood towards the lake and there is a crossing to the other side at a point where there is a descending stream on the right and a small lake on the left, with crags on each side. Cross over here, and follow the path round the northern side of the main lake to the far end. This is a beautiful spot with a combination of water, trees and crags, the most prominent crag across the lake being named Ravens Crag. During rhododendron time the area is particularly lovely, as it is also at the time of autumn colours.

On reaching the end of the lake, cross over, first along a narrow concrete walkway, then over a small hump bridge, to a rather wet path which leads to a waymarked path up the hill through the woods, terminating at a gate into fields on the hill top. Bear left across two fields towards Hollin Hill Farm. Turn left along the farm track, using an official diversion past the farm (on your right) and through a gate into a field. Immediately turn right by the holly hedge, to reach a ladder stile on the right in 30 yards.

The next objective is Gowbusk, which consists of two separate farms close together. Having crossed the ladder stile, turn left into and along a narrow grass field between hedges, noting waymarks on posts on the right. Continue forward to follow the hedge and ditch on the right to reach the first farm. Here it may well be very muddy but pass straight through the farm to an opening on the left beside a shed. Go through the opening towards the second farm but turn right through a gate to a track which leads to the road (again the B6265).

Turn left and go downhill for about 150 yards to a footpath sign on the right just before a group of buildings. Take this path, following the hedge on the left to a stile and then continuing to the top of the hill to reach a gateway beside a square concrete building. Here turn left over a waymarked stile and continue down the field, with a wall on the right, at the bottom of which is a fence stile into a little grass lane. This ascends to a waymarked fence stile at which turn left, down through a gateway, and with a hedge still on the left pass the end of the school at Sawley. A stone stile at the corner at the bottom of the field gives access to the village green and back to the car.

Grantley and Lumley Moor

There is plenty of variety in this walk – field paths, moorland tracks and a delightful lake in a woodland setting.

ONE mile to the north-west of Risplith, which is on the B6265 road, five miles from Ripon, six from Pateley Bridge, is the village of High Grantley. Park here near the telephone box. Walk past the chapel towards the old school; this is still in use and was founded as long ago as 1712. At the side of the school is a narrow tarmac lane which forks to the right. Walk up the lane until it bends sharply to the right. Go through the field gateway seen opposite and straight across the narrow field to a stone stile. Now walk alongside the hedge on the right, over a stile (or through the adjoining gate) and across the next field towards farm buildings at the left corner. Cross over a fence in the stone wall and pass directly between the buildings to the right hand of two gates, leading into a large field.

Follow the hedge line on the left until it turns away, and then cross by an isolated tree diagonally upwards to the top right-hand corner of the field where there is a stone stile. Over the stile go along the hedge then wall side towards the next group of buildings at the far end of the field. Here there are new cottages as well as farm buildings, but there is a marked right of way over the wall facing you and then straight alongside the back of the house to a lane.

Cross the lane to a stile and continue across the next field to a stile in the wall beside fencing, at which point bear diagonally right towards a gateway at the right hand end of a short wall ahead. Continue towards the farm buildings of Skelding Grange, and pass to the left of all the buildings to a stone stile which leads to a narrow lane, along which turn right. Keep in this lane to join the road which has come from Grantley and goes to Pateley Bridge. Walk forward along the road as far as the next corner. The route now goes straight ahead up the unmade lane, a public bridleway, called Drift Lane. Walk up this lane, which leads to Skelding Moor, for about half a mile. Cross a stream, the Holborn Beck, pass through a gate and follow the track up the moor to a group of rocks. This part of Skelding Moor is called Grange Allotment and the little mound only a few yards to the left of the track is worth a visit to secure a wide-sweeping view of the surrounding moorland. The wall on the right goes away from the track, so carry straight on, and eventually bear over towards the wall again, passing between two stone gateposts and reaching a gate at a junction of tracks.

It is worth noting here that the track ahead is Westhod Lane, which leads in half a mile to the road near the Drovers Inn, which would allow a connection to be made with the Dallowgill Walk. Altogether, this would make a figure of eight walk of 13½ miles, using Westhod Lane both ways.

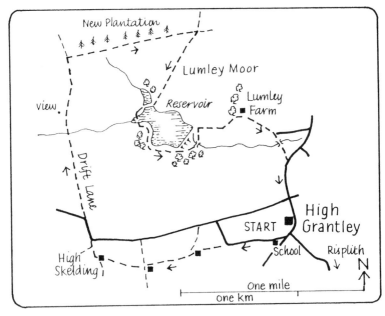

Pass through the gate and turn right on a wide green track with a wall on the right, and head towards the woodland, which is New Plantation, at which there is a gate. Pass through this gate and continue along the track at the edge of the woodland, with the wall still on the right. At the end of the wood continue forward for a short distance alongside a line of bushy trees, through a gate and beside another line of stubby trees to a waymarked stile over the wall on the right. (This stile is opposite a wall corner and a gate.)

This has brought us to Lumley Moor. Walk straight down the open moorland, at first keeping to the edge of the reedy area over to the right. Then pass through the reeds to a waymarked stile over a wire fence. Go forward in the same line of march, uphill towards a broken wall. The largest piece is actually a purpose-built stone cairn incorporating a yellow post waymark. Now aim towards the centre of the line of trees seen ahead which brings you to a yellow marked post at the edge of a reedy area. Bear left towards

16

the left-hand edge of the line of trees, to reach a wall stile over to Lumley Moor Reservoir.

This stretch of water is a very pleasant place at which to spend a little time, either to picnic or to observe the bird life or just to walk around and about.

From the stile go forward to cross between two parts of the reservoir, then turn left between hedges and pass between the stone parapets of a bridge over the Holborn Beck, which was crossed earlier in the walk and now enters the reservoir. There is now a wall on the right which is followed round on a woodland track to the dam. Go down to a wide grass track leading to a grassy terrace before some waterworks buildings. Cross a sluice and pass the buildings on a tarmac drive which joins the main drive. Turn right, pass the buildings of Lumley Farm and continue on the drive until it meets woodland. There is a stile here into the woods so follow the path down through them and over a rustic bridge to climb up through the woods on the other side. Go over a fence stile to a field and straight across it to a gate and a road. Turn right up the hill and walk back to the car, passing the Grantley Arms on the way.

Dallowgill

Green lanes, bridle tracks, wooded valleys and moorland make the Dallowgill area ideal walking country with a backcloth embracing Kirkby Malzeard, Carle Moor, Hambleton Hill and Dallowgill Moor.

ON the road north-east out of Pateley Bridge, north out of Glasshouses or west out of Ripon through Galphay, stands the modernised *Drovers Inn* (map reference 210720). Parking for walkers is not permitted at the inn, but there is just room for cars on the verge two fields to the south-west of the *Drovers* on the same side of the road. Walk along the road towards Laverton, taking the first turning to the left at the signpost indicating Dallowgill 1¼ (Pateley Bridge 7, Laverton 1¼, Kirkby Malzeard 2¼). Where the tarmac road turns left, go straight on – the road is marked "unsuitable for motors" and bears the ancient name of Belford Lane. Tarmac soon gives way to a double track which becomes a green lane on descending straight forward to the infant River Laver. Cross a footbridge and continue in a wet green lane (which can be avoided on the right), taking you on to Carlesmoor Beck. Turn left into another green lane and right at the end of it to a green track between hedges down to a ford and foot-bridge now crossing Carlesmoor Beck to enter Drift Lane, rising to the tarmac road from Kirkby Malzeard. Turn left and walk along the road for 200 yards turning right on a rough road signposted to "Carlsmoor" (without an "e" on this occasion).

It is worth pausing before turning. Straight ahead is the monument on Greygarth Hill which we shall eventually skirt round, to the right front is the ravine of Carlesmoor Beck and on the hillside above it is one of several sighting towers to be seen hereabouts. The metalled road (not tarred) descends to a bridge crossing Stock Beck in a delightful valley – Bagwith Brae is on the right – and is alongside Carlesmoor Beck, where the works and hut of the Leeds Water Authority may be seen on the left, before the track rises by the side of trees to Carlesmoor Farm. The track now passes the farm and ascends to a green lane, emerging on to a pasture to continue by the side of a wall on the left.

Passing through a gate on to the open moor, turn left on a stone track through heather, jump across the stream at a rocky ford and turn left on the track, which is soon to cross another stream. On returning to the tarmac road from Kirkby Malzeard, turn right and walk alongside as far as the guide post (Kirkby Malzeard 3½,

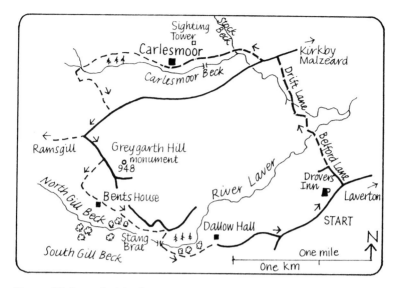

Ramsgill "unsuitable for motors" 4¾, and to the left Dallowgill 1¼). Take the Dallowgill road and 100 yards short of a cattle grid, leave the road and go through a gate on the right set at an angle.

(The monument on Greygarth Hill is to the left front from here, but there isn't a right of way to it.) There is, however, a path from the first gate on the left past the cattle grid. The edifice was erected in 1897 to commemorate Queen Victoria's Jubilee and was completely restored in 1984. The views from it are outstanding – to the east across the Vale of Mowbray to the Hambleton and Cleveland Hills and, to the west, to the bowl of the surrounding moorland. Below, the little chapel and cluster of dwellings indicate the hamlet of Greygarth.

Returning to the angled gate, a grassy track between walls leads downhill to fields and a succession of gates, with a wall on the right. Bearing left at the old farm buildings, pass through a small gate adjoining. Cross two fields to another gate on the immediate left of the next farm (Bents House) and then, with a wall on the right, pass through fields and gates on a bridleway which enters the top corner of the wood at Stang Brae. A clear track forward keeps just within the top edge of the wood until it forks. The right of way goes straight on, still just within the wood, to a gate. Go through it and cross the field diagonally in the same direction. Pass through a gate and turn right on a rough road. Descend through the wood to a concrete bridge or footbridge over North Gill Beck.

Walk up the road, taking the first turn left. Go through a gate and over South Gill Beck on another footbridge. Follow the broad track at first going uphill to the right to take you again into woods and continue on it to pass Dallow Cottages and Hall Farm, looking back from time to time for a view up the valley of North Gill Beck with Hambleton Hill (1,331 feet) at the head of it. Away beyond Greygarth Hill on the skyline of Grewelthorpe Moor (beyond Kirkby Malzeard Moor) may be seen the Sighting Tower standing at 1,178 feet. Leighton Reservoir is below (out of sight) and here is a link with one of the chapters of a companion volume to this book – *Walks in Wensleydale*. Pass one more farm and you soon reach the tarmac road. Turn left and you will be back at the starting point in a very short time.

Grewelthorpe and Hackfall

Leave Ripon from the Market Place by the Pateley Bridge road and take the very first turning to the right, signposted to Grewelthorpe. On entering the village note the village pond on the left and park as convenient to yourself and the villagers in the main street. Grewelthorpe is a village which will reward a short stay, but this could well be left to the end of the walk, as the return will include walking the length of the interesting village street.

There is much to be seen on the walk and many opportunities to wander and explore. The going is sometimes rough and, depending on the time of year, could well be muddy because of forestry activity. Ample time should be allowed for this is an outing which could well include a picnic.

TO start from the village pond walk back to the Ripon end of the street and note a footpath sign on the right hand side, pointing to a metal gate on the other side. This is the public footpath to Mickley and starts as a green lane between hedges. The lane goes through another gate and continues on, passing another lane on the left which has a waymark sign. After rising a little, there is a ruined building on the right and a further gate is reached by a holly hedge. This is the end of the lane, and the route goes over a fence stile on the right into a field.

Walk along the hedge line on the left to the corner where there is a waymarked fence stile into a field. Keep in line of march over the field to a waymarked fence stile in the hedge ahead, this stile being some 70 yards from the gate at the bottom right hand corner of the field. In the same direction cross over the next field to a waymarked fence stile near a gate, and keep forward to a dead tree less than 100 yards from the right hand corner of this field. Beside the tree is a waymarked fence post stile into a field. Continuing in the same direction make for a group of trees ahead to a waymarked stile and gate to the right of the trees. In the next field cross over to a post stile in the hedge facing you and then make towards the wall ahead, bearing right, leaving Bush Farm over to the right. Reach a gate in the corner, next to which there is an interesting waymarked stile to negotiate, and then continue forward and down some rough ground to step across a shallow stream and pass through a tiny stone stile. Now make for the left end of a line of trees ahead to join a track which leads into woodland, but turn right, away from the woodland along or beside a rough muddy track to reach the road at a footpath sign.

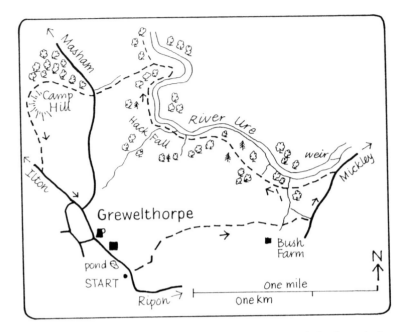

This road leads to Mickley and the route turns left along it for about a quarter of a mile. At a bend, where the road is descending, there is a seat next to a footpath sign stating 'Riverside Path', and at this point there is a beautiful view of the River Ure. The village of Mickley is about half a mile further on, and a diversion to see the village and the river by the old mill would be well worthwhile.

The riverside path goes into the woods, known as Mickley Barras, and more or less follows the course of the river for about a mile or so. Soon the path rises and then merges with the tracks of forestry vehicles. Cut straight over a cross forestry track on the woodland track which ascends as if to leave the river area. Do not take the rough vehicle track which descends towards the river but, beyond this, look for a well-defined woodland path on the right leading forward and into, and out of, an area of scrub and bracken. The twisting and winding path re-enters the woods and goes down to the part known as Hackfall. This part of the river is very beautiful and the water cascades over stones and rocks. Here there is a series of bends in the river; it is a very pleasant spot at which to picnic and from which to explore the woods.

A junction of tracks will be noted, particularly one leading up the side of a stream away from the river. This track leads up to the village of Grewelthorpe but is not a right of way, and there is a large notice at the top which states 'Private Woods. Trespassers will be prosecuted'. A series of steps will also be noticed up a short hill, which leads to a ruined pavilion of hexagonal shape, probably a summerhouse and observation point when it was built.

Our route continues onwards along the course of the river and provides especially good vistas of the Ure, although the walking may well be rough. A sandy beach may be seen at the riverside and an apparent path leading upwards on the left; this path should be ignored and you should continue to walk forward. After a little while the track swings away from the river, going up Limehouse Hill through the woods to meet and follow a wall upwards. At the end of the wall is a wicket gate and a fence, but continue upwards to reach a gate into a field. There is now a longish steep climb with a ditch, hedge and fence on the right, up to a gate and then to the road.

Emerging on the road at a footpath sign, turn left and cross over to an entry into forestry, which is Notwith Common. Walk straight up the forest drive and, as the main drive begins to bear to the right, note the wall going away on the left. Go over to the wall and join a path, keeping close to it. Walk along this path, with the wall on the left and a steep wooded slope on the right, to reach a wall corner. Continue round, with the wall on the left, and pass a gate, to continue following the wall to a waymarked wicket gate. Go through this gate and up the hill to a field gate at the top left. At this point look to the left to see a trig point on Horsepasture Hill, this being the highest point. Here also is the ancient earthwork of Camp Hill. The route now descends through pasture fields back to Grewelthorpe. With a hedge on your left, go over a step stile, then bearing right, go down to the right of a powerline post to a waymarked fence stile in the hedge ahead. Go straight across the next field to a waymarked fence stile to the right of another powerline post (at a right angle to the main line of posts) at a wall corner. Cross the next field diagonally down to the far corner, where the road is reached at a footpath sign.

Turn left along the road and, at the bottom of the hill, continue forward to the next junction, and then up the hill into Grewelthorpe past the Hack Fall Inn. Walking down the village street back to the car, there are several points of interest, amongst which are Grewelthorpe Handweavers who have a country shop, Mowbray Hall – reached from a lane by the side of the church, the Crown Inn, several vernacular buildings and the village pond.

Ilton Temple

Today's walk is only short, but it could be combined with a fine motor ride on the narrow road over the moors to Lofthouse in Nidderdale (via Leighton), or a visit to Masham, with its air of repose, dignified houses, lovely old church with a spire and spacious marketplace. Near Masham is Swinton Park, the home of the Earl of Swinton, and on the Swinton estate, between Ilton and Healey, is a pseudo druidical temple, worth a visit itself and for the fine viewpoint nearby. The building of the temple provided occupation for tenants and estate workmen early in the 19th century during a time of distress. The temple lies in Druid's Plantation, to the west of the Ilton/Healey road. A 'No Through Road' sign marks the end of Knowle Lane, leading to the temple. A Forestry Commission sign shows F.R.P. No. 2, and another 'Jervaulx Forest – Druid's Wood'.

IF all members of the party intend to walk 3½ miles there is no need to take the car further, but at the end of the lane is a fine car park and picnic place, laid out with benches and litter bags. If you prefer to leave the temple to the end of the journey, it should not be difficult to reverse the proposed route, but those intending to follow the clockwise journey as shown on the map go through the gate beside the main gate. Immediately in front is a notice which reads: 'Footpath to Druid's Temple by invitation of the Swinton Estate and Forestry Commission'. You could save a quarter of a mile by going straight ahead on the hard road; or you could make more of a walk of it by taking the alternative route left, which circles round to the viewpoint, marked by upright stones. Here one can see Leighton Reservoir, supplying water for Leeds; Colsterdale is beyond it; and on the skyline is Great Haw, with Little Haw to the right of it and another Little Haw (or South Haw) on the left.

Turn right to visit the temple, which is in sight, comprising an ovoid of stones with upright stones in the middle, a circle and a tomb. The twelve signs of the zodiac are portrayed on the high structure on the hill. To continue along the gravel road would return you to the picnic place. Those going further should take the wide green track forward on the left. Bear left at the first cross tracks on a path covered with pine needles, soon reaching the edge of the wood, with open views on the right of the Hambleton Hills. Continue to the gate at the opposite side of the wood; from here, keep to the trees in the same line of march to come to an opening in the narrow belt of woodland (through which a cart track passes of Low Knowle Farm). Keep going down hill and, after about a hundred yards, join a tractor trail steeply swooping to a gate.

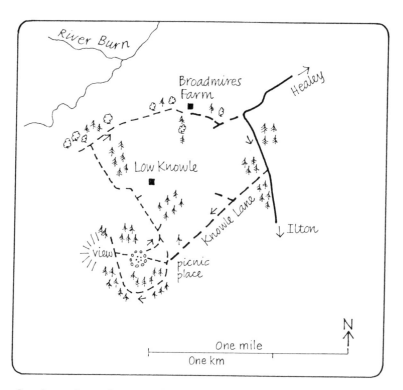

Continue through a gap in the next hedge to the wood at the bottom of the hill, turn right, pass through a gateway at the bottom right-hand corner of the field, and follow a tractor trail through green pastures.

On the left is the valley of the river Burn; across the dale the village of Healey. Pass to the right of the buildings of Broadmores Farm, joining the farm road out to the narrow tarred road by a wood side, and take the next turn to the right to bring you back to the car at one end of Knowle Lane or the other.

Colsterdale and Witton Fell

*The many charming features of Colsterdale are not so well known
as they should be. It was famous in the First World War for the
training camp of the Leeds Pals, the 15th Battalion, West Yorkshire
Regiment, who on 1st July, 1916, suffered crippling casualties in
the first Battle of the Somme. The camp was situated near Breary
Bank, on the other side of the river from today's starting point.*

LEAVE the car at Gollinglith Foot, near a telephone box beside
the delectable river Burn, reached from Masham through Healey
on the Colsterdale road. Those wishing to do the shorter version
of the walk should continue up valley to get as near as possible to
Slipstone Crags for a simple outward walk to Witton Fell and return
as described below. Motorists approaching from Wensleydale or
the north could use the alternative start from Stark Bank, near
Ellerstring.

Leaving the riverside, walk up the track signposted to Low
Agra, passing to the left of farm buildings and through a gate.
Continue on the stony track through pasture and, after passing
through a gate near Low Agra, keep near the boundary wall of the
woods on the right to a gate in the wall between two plantations.
Go straight up on good grass and make for the top left corner of
the field. Agra Farm is away on your right. On a cart-way keep
to the edge of a small conifer wood, towards the end of which go
through an opening in the wall on your left and turn half right in
the field to a gate in the cross wall. Now in an expansive pasture,
make to the left of a single pine tree for a gate in the wall beyond,
reaching a depression before it, where a clear track takes you to a
foot-bridge and up to the gate. Leighton Reservoir can be seen
on the right.

Continue in the line of march through heather on a faint track
which, after passing marshy ground in a dip, eventually leads to the
wall on the left – the parish boundary – let into which are several
boundary stones. The first stone reached bears 'Mashamshire' on
the near side and 'East Witton' on the far. Just beyond it, go over
a wooden stile, turn right and continue alongside the boundary
wall, where the right-of-way goes straight down to the Ellingstring
road. Two tracks on the left, not marked on the map as rights-of-
way at the time of writing, lead respectively to Moor Cote Farm
and Stark Bank top, to which the tarred road from Ellingstring
also leads. Below is the river Ure with Jervaulx on this side of it
and Thornton Steward on the other. Away to the right, over the

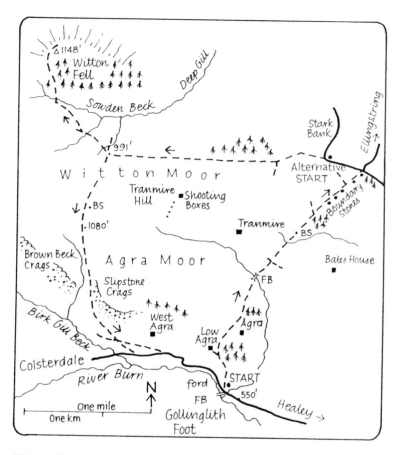

Vale of Mowbray, are the Hambleton Hills with the Clevelands to the north of them.

Join the metalled farm road leaving the corner of the tarmac road – the alternative starting point – and follow the main track past Moor Cote Farm, with its chalet roof. At the gate near the trees bear right on a well marked moorland track (sometimes muddy) with a conifer plantation on the right. The tree-covered objective of Witton Fell soon comes into sight to the right front, and when the view to the right opens out Leyburn can be seen across Wensleydale.

Coming down to a dip with a stream at the bottom, note a track to the left opposite a gate. We shall return to this point after climbing steadily to the top of Witton Fell, a mile away. Crossing the stream, the track soon leaves the side of the wall and makes

27

for an isolated stunted pine tree; nearing it, go to the pound on the right (guarding a waterworks stop valve) and follow animal tracks leading towards a gate in the wall protecting Witton Fell Plantation. Cross the ravine of Snowden Beck – which becomes Deep Gill Beck lower down, visited on Walk 8 – at a point opposite the gate, above some stream-side trees. A track through bracken and heather leads to the gate.

Keep to the woodland ride as far as a three-way junction. Bear right for no more than forty yards where on the left you will find a narrow footpath; take it. Trees have recently been blown down, partly obscuring the track, so care must be taken. After a quarter of a mile on this narrow track look on the right for a track leading to a triangulation pillar fifteen yards away, which can easily be missed as the angle of the side track is acute. Some 85 yards further on the trees thin out on the left, above some crags, where the view is superb. Middle and Lower Wensleydale stretch out before you, from Castle Bolton to the Vale of Mowbray. Another castle – Middleham – is below on the left; and the village of East Witton is on the right with the river Ure snaking towards Jervaulx and beyond.

Take the same path out of the wood, retracing steps across Witton Moor, and keep in the direction of the shooting house on the skyline – on Tranmire Hill. After rejoining the wall, now on the left, and crossing the stream, turn right along the tractor trail opposite the gate in the wall. The track goes between the second and third of a line of butts and passes to the right of a boundary stone marked 'A' on the opposite side; you are now on Agra Moor. To the right front, about four miles away, are from right to left Little Haw, 1,639 feet; Great Haw, 1,786 feet; Little or South Haw, 1,596 feet; and the pimple at the end of Brown Ridge, Throstle Hill, 1,562 feet. Behind Great Haw, 7½ miles from where we are walking, is Little Whernside, 1,984 feet.

Colsterdale now opens out in front, the track going quickly down by Slipstone Crags, an impressive rock formation. On the other side of the ravine, going away on the right, are Brown Beck Crags. On passing through the gate at the foot of the track keep to the left-hand green track by the wall on your left, on springy turf beside bracken and gorse. Join the road leading from West Agra Farm. Below are large pipes crossing the river Burn taking water from the catchment area to Leighton Reservoir and, eventually, to Leeds. The reservoir is on the other side of the hill behind the red house seen ahead. The road takes a sharp bend down to the river at a gate marked 'Boddy Close'. Those electing to do the shorter return journey may choose to leave the car here. A pleasant stroll down the road, or round the bends of the river, brings one back to Gollinglith Foot.

Jervaulx Abbey and
the River Ure

*Jervaulx is situated on the main road to Wensleydale from Ripon,
five miles from Masham and three from Middleham. The Cistercian
abbey was founded by monks who came to the site from Fors in
1147.*

*They bred horses and were reputed to have discovered the recipe
for making Wensleydale cheese. Only the outline of the 13th century
church remains, built up of stones from the other parts of the abbey.
The 12th century lay brothers' range is still to be seen; also the 14th
century abbot's lodge, 15th century infirmary, chapter house and
cloister. The buildings and grounds, privately owned, are open to
the public on weekdays from 10 a.m. to 6 p.m.*

PARK the car in the car park opposite the abbey. Those wishing
to walk on routes A, B or C go downhill along the main road for
300 yards and, immediately after passing over Lea Gill Beck, turn
right on a tractor trail by the side of the stream which soon leads to
the river Ure – broad, fast-flowing, stony in parts and often tree-
lined. The path to the left all the way to Cover Bridge is easily
followed by the riverside, passing a fish pond on the left and Danby
Park on the other side of the river. It is pleasant to linger by the
weir beside Danby Low Mill, now disused, and to observe the first
of three tree-covered islands called The Batts. Passing through a
gate the track is now beside the river Cover, narrower and swifter
than the Ure, leading to the shapely Cover Bridge. The Inn, quaint
and popular with fishermen, was established in 1674. Route C
walkers are recommended to return here along the riverside, the
main road being further and more dangerous.

Routes A and B walkers cross the road, descend five stone steps
and immediately cross two stiles to come again to the river Cover.
Continue walking beside it on the outside of a fence, make for a
gap in the hedge ahead and go through a gate in the next hedge.
Cut across the field to a barn, at the far side of which is a 'V' stile
in the field wall. Turn left at the other side. Keep the wall on your
left all the way to the foot of the hill below East Witton. Do not go
through the gate on the left, but continue forward over a stile, the
boundary on your immediate left now being a fence and hedge.
Enter a small field, leaving it by a stile in the far left-hand corner.
Pass through a paddock and arrive at the village through a small
gate on the right of the Methodist chapel.

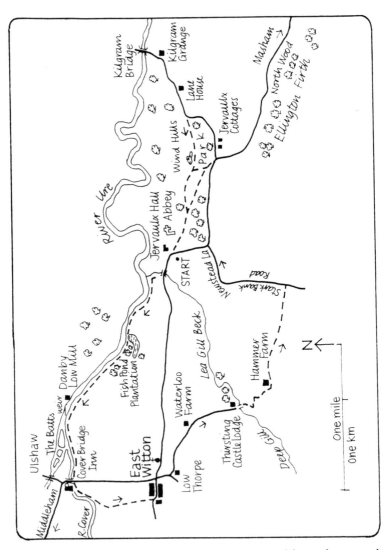

East Witton comprises an elongated green with roads on each side and neat, regular cottages. Turn left towards the church but, on reaching the main road, take the narrow road on the right through Low Thorpe, bearing left at the fork. Pass the graveyard of the former St. Martin's church and go to the right of Waterloo Farm and its blue silo. Keep to the tarmac road on a sharp, uphill climb at the top of which, beyond Thirsting Castle Lodge – where the dogs will bark – the tarmac expires. The track goes over a rushing stream, Deep Gill Beck on the right which becomes Lea Gill Beck on the left, and into a field.

Leave the field by a gate near the top right-hand corner, taking a zig-zag track uphill. At the end of the first 'zig' the track forks – take the right-hand track to a post and wire fence, turn left and take the first gate on the right, keeping a double fence on your left. Go through two gates in quick succession on your left and make for the right-hand side of Hammer Farm, picking up the farm road in front of the house. After passing over a stream on a cattle grid, the farm road goes into a lane which leads to the narrow, tarmac Stark Bank Road. Turn left on the road which leads down to Newstead Lane and out on to the main road. Route B walkers turn left here and you will soon be back at Jervaulx.

Route A walkers, instead of returning to the car park, turn right and walk on the busy main road (single file on the right-hand side recommended) for a little more than half a mile. Jervaulx Abbey Park is on the left. Where the main road turns right for Masham, opposite the park gate, keep straight on, passing Jervaulx Cottages and, now on a minor road, continue to Kilgram Bridge said by some writers to be the eastern boundary of Wensleydale. It is a fine bridge, over the wide river Ure, with a raised trod above flood level at the far side.

Return along this minor road as far as the lodge on the right at a bend. A sign tells you the drive is a private road, but there is a right of way for walkers on the road through the park, hilly with drumlins (glacial deposits) and well laid out with clumps of trees. Pass a lake and a small pond, observe the abbey on the right, and leave the grounds by the footpath to a signpost by the roadside. The car park is almost opposite.

Strollers on route D should go into the park at the signpost (which reads 'to the Abbey') and take the main drive until nearly opposite the fine house, Abbey Hill, on the right. Take the footpath leading to the gates near Jervaulx Cottages; turn left on the road to follow Kilgram Lane as far as the lodge on the left; and go over the cattle grid and into the park as described above. The right of way through the park applies only to the two routes mentioned. All other tracks are private.

Upper Wensleydale

FORMERLY called Yoredale or Uredale – the river gave it its name – the wide, green, wooded upper Wensleydale is distinctive for its size and beauty, famous for its cheese, and perhaps better known to road users than to pedestrians, although the five-pronged head of the dale has long been favourite walking country. Now that the Pennine Way passes through the dale, ramblers know it even better. The motorist's best broad picture of Wensleydale is probably from Scarth Nick on Preston Scar, above Redmire. Those arriving from the north-east will see Penhill across the valley, Bishopdale to its right, and then the head of the dale, lying to the right of the distinctive shape of the hill called Addlebrough. In between, the river Ure snakes through beautifully wooded country. Approaching from Masham, a good general view is obtained by walking up Witton Fell (see Walk 7). On the other side can be seen the terraced hills and scars of the Yoredale Series of limestones. This vantage point also gives a reminder of the place of Wensleydale in history. Below is Middleham Castle, associated with Richard III. Bolton Castle – ancestral home of the Scropes – is in the middle distance, and Jervaulx Abbey is away to the right.

The head of the dale is on the Cumbria and North Yorkshire border at Hell Gill. Almost certainly, the party bringing Mary Queen of Scots to her imprisonment in Bolton Castle would pass over Hell Gill Bridge and first see Wensleydale on the old High Way, now a green track. But it is the Pennine wayfarers, travelling northwards, whose first look at the dale from Ten End Fell, gives them the finest comprehensive view to the east, embracing the whole of this lovely region.

The foot of the upper dale is not so well defined as its head. In its turn Wensley Bridge has been suggested. Wensley, now a small village of exquisite charm, was once a market town, giving its name to the dale. Bolton Hall – the seat of Lord Bolton – is here, its wooded parkland contributing so much to the character of this part of the dale. Cover Bridge, beloved by fishermen, has also been proffered as the dale end. Still lower down the river, Kilgram Bridge may be taken as the boundary. But who can dispute it if the dwellers of Bedale and Masham claim to live in Wensleydale?

Waterfalls, caused by the differing resistance to weathering of limestone and shale, are a constant delight in the side valleys of this 'family of dales'. But the most famous are at Aysgarth. Also in the main valley is Hardraw Force, 99 feet high, England's highest fall above ground.

A big geological influence upon the shape of Wensleydale was the Ice Age. U-shaped valleys were gouged out by glaciers and in these flat valley bottoms lakes appeared when the meltwaters were dammed by moraines. Semerwater, one of Yorkshire's few natural lakes, is the only one remaining in the dale. Drumlins – well-moulded humps of rock debris and boulder clay – are conspicuous, especially in the area above Aysgarth.

My first experience of Wensleydale was on a schoolboy cycling tour, travelling down-dale from Widdale and Hawes. It was Whit Sunday; the slanting sun gave ethereal beauty to the fells and woodlands ahead of us; the calm evening, a slight following wind, and the downward slope gave us freewheeling pleasure. Ringing across the vale as we sped silently on the uncluttered road, church bells added the final touch of peace and tranquility. The memory of those moments has stayed with me for more than half a century. On today's busy roads it would be difficult to repeat the experience, but similar harmony can arise on foot in the hills and valleys – especially at the end of a day on the tops. It is my wish that such moments may fall to your lot.

Great Haw

Coverdale, the lovely valley of the river Cover (to rhyme with 'hover'), offers many good walks, up hill and down dale. The intention today is to climb a gentle thousand feet – or nearly so. The charming ride along the narrow Braithwaite Lane from East Witton takes one past Coverham Bridge. On the other side of the river is Coverham Abbey, now a farm with little left to see of the old monastery. Do not cross the bridge but continue by car to West Scrafton where there is a parking place on the road side just before the houses.

ON entering the village there is a bridge over the rushing stream of Great Gill with a gate by the side of it. Go uphill with the stream on your right and a modernised country house on your left. The track soon leaves the beck and curls uphill on the right-hand side of a wall ceasing to be in somewhat muddy condition and becoming a smooth green track through tufted grass, never more than 100 yards from the wall until this turns away and our track turns right, sloping uphill. Before taking this turn note the crags ahead with an anvil shaped stone on top – Great Roova.

Walking up the long but gradual slope, notice across the marshy ground on the right a cleft in the moor, showing the line of the return journey. Pass an automatic ram for pumping water on the left and, a little further on, Roova Pot Hole fifty feet uphill (and therefore to be searched for). Next come spoil heaps from some old, small, drift coal mines – narrow seams of coal were mined in the Dales, chiefly in the late eighteenth and early nineteenth centuries.

Cross a small stream, headed by Great Bank Well; the path is reduced to a single track going on to a deep gully with a natural bridge over the stream. If you reach this point you have been led beyond the official track, which you can soon regain by following the stream upwards to the big spoil heap, enclosed by a fence protecting animals – and you – from the wide circular shaft of a coal mine. The lip of the shaft is crumbly and insecure – so be warned! Between the mine and a post and wire fence, seen ahead, is some rather boggy ground. Cross this to a gate in the fence where we leave the right of way to turn right, following the parish boundary which can be seen stretching from Great and Little Roova Crags, on the left, to our objective today, on the right, to and beyond it. Animal tracks go through the tufted grass on our side of the fence, and through the heather on the other. From here, in clear weather, the 'table top' of Little Whernside can

34

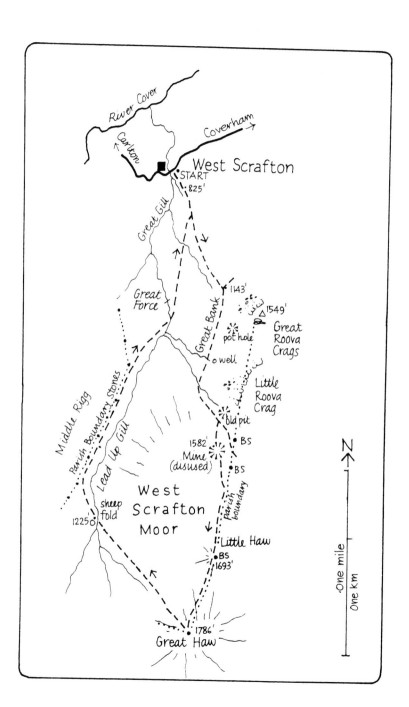

River Cover

Carlton

Coverham →

West Scrafton

START
825'

Great Gill

1143'

Great Force

Great Bank

△ 1549'

pot hole

o well

Great Roova Crags

Little Roova Crag

old pit

BS

1582'
Mine (disused)

BS

Middle Rigg

Parish Boundary Stones

Lead Up Gill

Parish boundary

West Scrafton Moor

sheep fold

1225'

Little Haw

BS
1693'

1786'
Great Haw

N ↑

One mile

One km

35

be seen to the right front, as we advance, with Great Whernside going away from it.

About half a mile from where the fence was joined, another gate is reached – on some slightly higher ground. Notice that one of the gateposts is a boundary stone; this is Little Haw. The gills starting from the moor top on the left go down into Colsterdale, and straight ahead is Great Haw. On the way to it there was once another gate, which was on the right of way we shall pick up on the return from the top, a quarter of a mile further on, where our fence meets the fence of the old county boundary. A boundary stone will be seen where this gate stood, with the words 'Danby-Mashamshire' inscribed on it. For views of Nidderdale it is necessary to continue in the line of march on the other side of the fence. The boundary to the left front goes down to the other Little Haw (or South Haw).

Retrace your steps from the fence junction for about a quarter of a mile and then bear to the left at an angle of about 50 degrees to the fence towards the right-hand nick of two which should be seen at the edge of the moor. Although there is a right of way (from Nidderdale) there is no well-trodden footpath on the top of the moor. Animal tracks should, however, help to take you through the tufted grass towards the moor edge (this is West Scrafton Moor), but leave the track which continues along the edge so as to reach the brow of the moor at a point just to the right of a gill.

Down below you should see a sheep fold, immediately below the junction of Lead Up Gill and the side beck. Go to it. Descending the grass becomes smooth beneath the feet but on reaching bracken you should with luck find a grassy path down to the stream. Cross it before coming to the fold and you will soon pass the foundations of an old building – marked 'shooting house' on the 2½ inch map. Now there is a path going up to the boundary fence on the left – on the Middle Rigg – from which there are views of the length of Coverdale on the left with the two Whernsides at its head. Follow the line of boundary stones until they bear off to the left. At this point make for the stream which is crossed within a hundred yards of the wall end. It can be pleasant to linger here, where the water falls over a series of little ledges – although a few hundred yards lower down is the more dramatic Great Force, the second of two waterfalls, well worth making one of the objectives of this walk.

The official track takes a short sharp pull up from the stream crossing and levels off, gradually moving away from the beck across ground – sometimes marshy – between two walls, eventually joining the outward track which runs alongside the right-hand wall. On the left, across Coverdale, is Penhill which will be climbed on Walk 10. To the left of Penhill is Harland Hill which will be encircled on Walk 11. Less than 500 yards of descent, after joining the outward track, brings you back to West Scrafton.

Penhill

Travellers in the Vale of Mowbray or on the Hambleton Hills must often have looked to the west to identify Wensleydale by its jaws, especially the southern 'jaw', Penhill – a miniature Ingleborough – bounded by Coverdale, Walden, and Wensleydale.

THE plan is a simple one, put in especially for those who like to get on the tops without too much exertion! The more energetic could quite easily combine it with Walk 11 by using the parish boundary over the Height of Hazely, the west height of Penhill, but it should be remembered that the right of way stops opposite Black Scar. The short journey is to the Beacon, 1,685 feet above sea level – but the start will be from 1,175 feet. On the narrow road between West Witton and Melmerby is a cattle grid where the enclosed road goes on to Middleham High Moor (which provides the summer gallops for racehorses from many stables). A hundred yards downhill from the cattle grid is a gateway on the Penhill side of the road and a wide grass verge on which to park. There is also a convenient parking area just above the cattle grid.

From the gateway there is a track, which keeps to the brow of the hill through fields and a number of gates, heading straight for the Beacon visible at the top of Penhill. Take it, and emerging from the fields on to the moor you should see on your right, from right to left: the village of Wensley in a lovely setting; Bolton Hall and parkland; Preston-under-Scar, suitably named; Redmire; and Castle Bolton above and to the left, with the distinctive shape of Bolton Castle beyond the village. Passing through a moorland gate, the track takes on a new shape with ditches on each side. It curves round to the left of the steep hillside and 200 yards further on reaches a thorn tree a few feet below on the left, marking Robin Hood's Well which exudes clear refreshing water. It is easy to miss the thorn tree, so do not rely on this as a convenient way-mark. Continue upwards on the track for about 100 yards and then turn right across the moat to scramble up the square stone cairn which marks the site of the Beacon. One can imagine a fire being lit here when news was received of the defeat of the Spanish Armada. West Witton can now be seen below in Wensleydale, while on the other side, looking across Coverdale, on the left is Witton Moor (not unlike Penhill), then come Little and Great Haw and over to the right are Little and Great Whernside.

Take the green track through tufted grass and heather, keeping to the Wensleydale edge of the moor – the caravans below tend to

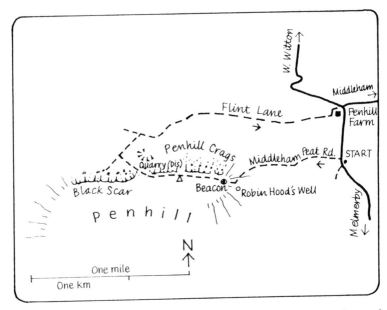

spoil the picture, but the site is well concealed from the main road and West Witton village. Pass to the right of a round barrow, with an upright stone on top, and along the top of the tall Penhill Crags as far as a slit stile in a wall across the path. Those who do not seek a scramble down the grassy slope between Penhill Crags and Black Scar, which can be dangerous in winter weather, may consider returning to the car from here by making an about turn. Another complication is that although we intend to join a right of way down below, the link between is open ground with no public path shown on the map.

Continuing beyond the stile, the shapely form of Addlebrough can be seen ahead on the other side of Bishopdale. After negotiating a wire fence – the wire near the wall on the right is not barbed – walk for 100 yards or so along the cliff edge. The crags end here and the steep grass slope can be descended to join tracks among old workings and through a pasture to a gate at the right-hand bottom corner. Turn right at the other side and walk on the left of a wall to another gate which leads to the walled Flint Lane – a green lane from which there are more good views of Wensleydale. This in turn joins the narrow tarmac road above West Witton. Turn right and walk uphill to the starting point.

Coverdale and Walden

Using two ancient bridleways between the lovely valleys of Coverdale and Walden, the walker completely encircles Harland Hill – an extension of Penhill – and climbs fairly gently to heights giving fine vistas of the surrounding country. The walk may begin either from Cote Bridge in Walden, or if one finds oneself in Coverdale, from half a mile west of Carlton.

WE start from the former, taking us through the well-kept village of West Burton, which has some fine houses, a compact green and a delightful waterfall. At the top of the village, bear left in the car, passing the 'No Through Road' sign and taking the road for Walden South. Go gently over the hump-back Cote Bridge, where there is a caravan site, and park on the wide verge or on the triangle of grass 200 yards beyond the bridge.

Walk up the stony track, passing to the left of a square chimney. To regain breath, pause at the first gate to look back. Beyond Walden is Bishopdale, and further west Addlebrough stands above the general line of the hills. The village on the other side of Wensleydale is Carperby, with some of the easterly houses of Aysgarth in between. Past the end of a wall the stony track turns temporarily to the right; either keep to it or cut off a corner by going forward up the hill. Do not be tempted to the track by the fence lower down on the left, but make the stiffish climb through bracken, bearing right until the track – now green and cropped – is regained. The path clings more or less to a stone wall on the left, but leave this when it turns away and continue in the same direction – or slightly to the right to avoid some marshy ground.

Very soon you will see the parish boundary wall. Turn left on a green double track before it, crossing the line of march, and right after a few yards on a single track which soon becomes double. Go through a gateway in the boundary wall, turn immediately to the right and, after a few yards, bear left and follow a double green track crossing enclosed land. Now we are looking into Coverdale; the track reaches the wall on the right and keeps to it until passing out of the enclosure at a gap in the next wall. Keep straight forward on a green track, going downhill parallel to a gill on the left. As Howden Lodge comes into sight, take stock of the hills on the other side of Coverdale, from Witton Fell on the left past Roova Crags, Little and Great Haw, to Little Whernside on the right – Great Whernside will also soon come into view.

Pass immediately to the left of the now deserted house; the deep drift on the left is Howden Scar. Keeping Howden Scar on your left, join a tractor trail along a line of shooting butts – a green, heathery, gravelly track which brings you to two gates at the junction of walls. Take the left-hand one, turning squarely; go through another gate on to a green track between a wall and a barbed wire fence, and continue downhill on a track between walls which meets a narrow tarmac road. Turn right through a metal gate.

People starting from Coverdale should leave the car here on the wide grass verge, having taken the narrow uphill road, marked 'unsuitable for motors', out of the top end of the village of Carlton. It turns left to go up the dale; park at the end of the tarred road. The road is still shown as untarred in the current editions of O.S. maps. Walk through the gate straight ahead.

On a good farm road go through a wooden gate, passing in front of the farm, and then an iron gate beyond. The road turns left in the direction of another farm but go straight on, passing through a wooden gate and keeping a wall on your left. Go through a second gate and then a gap – often muddy – in a wall. Step across a tributary of Turn Beck and then through a gate immediately beyond. Turn right, keeping the wall on your right; when you reach the end of this wall look for a gate ahead and pass through it. Go down to Turn Beck, crossing it over stepping stones to a gate. Bear to the right along the depression of an ancient track following the stream in which there is a succession of pleasant little waterfalls. By keeping just above stream level you see ahead a gate – go through it.

The hollow to the right front is Cumma Bottom. Underfoot the grass is tufted; on the left is a conifer plantation – keep about 200 yards away from it in order to be on the right of way and to dodge a depression ahead. When you reach a wall across your path you have a problem. The official footpath passes through it 200 yards from the edge of the wood but when last visited there were no signs of gap, gate or stile – and the wall has many loose stones in it. This can be overcome by going down to the copse (off the right of way), crossing the wall using a step stone in the corner and passing through a gate about 150 yards along another wall (on your left). Cross the next field diagonally to join a farm road which takes you through the next plantation, regaining the right of way. Continue to a tarmac road just in front of Fleensop Farm house. Turn left over a bridge, and 300 yards later go through a gate set at an angle on the right.

Do not stay too long on the cart road in the field but go uphill to a gate in the top left-hand corner. On the open moor keep to the right of a wall, veering away from it when you see a post on the ridge by the side of another wall. A notice says 'Bridle road of Walden...'; we follow this to the right, leaving the Horsehouse bridle road. Keep the wall on your left for just under a mile,

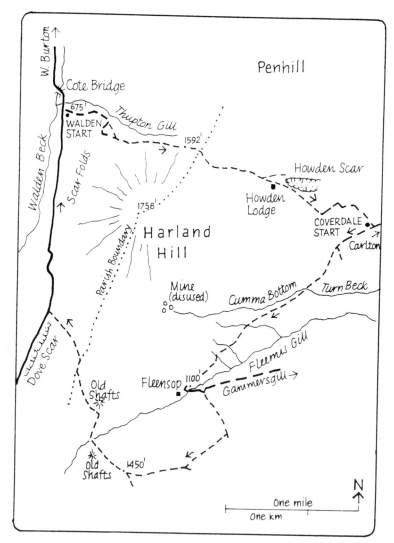

opposite a stile, turn half right away from it on a clear track. Pass a white-topped post – and another one – before reaching a wall across the path which bears to the right to a green gate.

Turn right on a double track on the other side and pass some old coal mines. Going down to the stream, look to the right for a good view of Fleemis Gill which was crossed at Fleensop. Notice, in dry weather, that the water of the beck disappears into the ground at the foot of a waterfall. Keep to the main track on the other side

41

and go through a gate; at a fork a guide post indicates the way, bearing left to West Burton and Aysgarth (it also shows we are on the Horsehouse bridleway). Look to the left for Buckden Pike coming into sight; then go through another gate in the boundary wall (passed earlier in the day on the other side of Harland Hill). Descending into Walden, the hill on the other side of the dale is Wasset Fell. Pass through another gate and by the side of an old railway luggage van to join the narrow tarmac road at a signpost which indicates we have come from the direction of Horsehouse and Kettlewell and tells us the way to West Burton. A mile of walking on the quiet road above the delightful Walden Beck finishes the journey of those who elected to start from Cote Bridge.

Walden Beck and Buckden Pike

Buckden Pike dominates the whole valley of Walden. It is one of the highest peaks in the Yorkshire Pennines but 'Pike' is a misnomer: its top is bulky but not sharp. Well-trodden tracks go over the fell from Wharfedale side – not all rights of way – but the ancient bridleway from Walden Head to Starbotton is not much walked upon these days, although we shall use it. Do not be deceived by the short distance; five hours could easily be taken over the longer journey, if time is allowed for rests and admiration of the views. It is not a casual stroll and walkers should be properly shod, clad and provisioned.

WALDEN Beck is delightful and well worth a visit – at least as far as the first waterfall – and one can return via Groove End if a little climbing is acceptable. Motor nearly to Walden Head via West Burton where one takes the 'No through road' and the turn to Walden North. The tarmac road ends at Kentucky House, the last farm on the left; just before it there is room for parking three or four cars on the grass verge. Continue on foot from here up the dale, past the farm, after which the road becomes a track crossing the stream on a wooden bridge.

In recent years the old bridleway from Walden to Starbotton has been diverted from the east to the west bank of the beck at this point. Walkers now cross the bridge and immediately turn left to follow a path running close to the edge of the beck. After about half a mile it becomes a green tractor trail running along the valley floor. Go over the Deepdale Beck on smooth rock and soon you will see that the main stream on the left has gone underground; here you can cross to a well-used sheep track on the other side and re-cross above the next junction to walk between two streams for a hundred yards or so. Those intending to follow B route should return to this place after continuing upstream.

B walkers, having returned from seeing the first waterfall (the biggest and best), turn up the side valley at the end of which they will see steep cliffs. This little dale is also delightful. Before reaching the cliffs leave the stream side and climb up the hillside on the right to join the right of way at the top – on Groove End. Turn right on sheep tracks, which abound, and when presented with alternatives take the track on the right unless it is obviously going down into the valley. The right of way is over the hump of Groove End, rejoining the Deepdale Beck where it was crossed on the outward trip. Retrace your steps to your point of departure.

Route A walkers continue up the main gill, very soon reaching a series of rocky cascades, one drop being particularly impressive. Above the fall the water passes over some flat rocks and beneath the high crags of Raven Scar. Scramble up by the side of the beck, crossing and recrossing, until you come to the last of the falls. This one has less water going over it and is mossy. Climb up the drift on the left of the fall (as you face it); if you turn round and look back you see Brown Haw, 1,904 feet, part of North Moor. Above the waterfall the parish boundary fence may be seen on the skyline on the left; straight ahead, and to the right front, are signs of the old county boundary wall. These enclosures are somewhat comforting if one is caught in mist – the trail may be picked up by turning to the right on reaching one boundary or the other. Pit spoil heaps may also be seen towards the skyline to the right front; make for them, using water courses which are easier walking than the heather and tufted grass of the moor.

At the first division of water above the fall, take the main course on the left-hand side for a simple route to the pits. Look back, when the stream becomes merely a trickle, down the dale of Walden and beyond Brown Haw for a sight of Harland Hill and the back of Penhill. On the left-hand side of the valley is Noughtberry Hill. Looking east, notice the shape of Little Whernside – not such a tableland as when seen from the opposite direction. At the old quarries shelter can be found within carefully constructed walls. Here also is the unmistakable path of the right of way, which somewhat unusually is clearly seen. We shall pick it up later on, returning from the top, but its position may then have to be judged rather than seen.

From the quarries it is only a quarter of a mile to the county boundary wall across rough country. Make for it at its nearest point in order to join the beaten track by the side of the wall. Turn right on springy peat – Wharfedale and Littondale are below on the left; behind is Great Whernside, now seen as a continuation of Little Whernside. Very soon you should come to a cross reading 'Thanksgiving to God. The Parker family and local people. In memory of five Polish R.A.F. airmen who died here on 31.1.42 – buried in Newark – the survivor.' The date at the foot of the cross is August 5th, 1973.

On the other side of the wall you are in the old West Riding, now part of North Yorkshire. From here there is a good view of Penyghent, with its 'lion's head' facing towards the left; flat-topped Ingleborough is behind and Whernside, less recognisable, appears at the head of the valley which goes away in front of you – Langstrothdale Chase. Continuing along the side of the wall, you soon arrive at the cairn and trig. point at the top of Buckden Pike. Below on the left is the minor road leading to the track over Stake Moss to Semerwater; looking in the same direction there is the Kidstones Pass taking the road from Wharfedale into Bishopdale

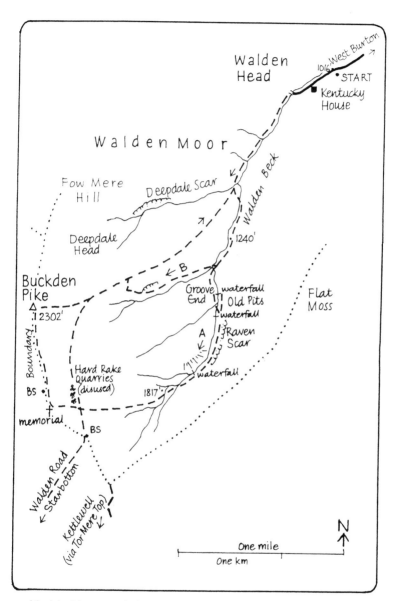

and behind is a good view of the U-shaped glacial dale of Walden, with Walden Head indicating the point of return.

Leave the top on a track at right angles to the wall – the pits should be seen on the right. We join the right of way which comes from the pits, curving in front of us towards Groove End. You will not find a continuous track; walk between peat hags in the general direction of the pump of Groove End – or Walden Head in clear conditions. Pass some shallow pot holes, using sheep tracks dropping down to the spur ahead, where you should pick up a tractor trail leading to Deepdale Beck and the main stream. This must be crossed before reaching the plantation ahead, thus enabling you to retrace your steps to the starting point beyond Kentucky House.

Bolton Castle and Apedale

Probably the most easily recognised feature in Wensleydale is the square keep of Bolton Castle; maybe the least-known is Apedale, so today we shall combine the two. The shorter walk involves motoring from the castle to the second guide post on the Grinton road and taking the walk along the rough track to Dent's Houses and back.

QUOTING from *The Yorkshire Dales* by Marie Hartley and Joan Ingilby, 'Bolton Castle is owned by Lord Bolton, and is open to the public. It was built by Richard Scrope, first Lord Scrope, Chancellor of England, who in 1379 obtained licence to crenellate his manor house; some details of its erection and construction are recorded by Leland. From 13th July 1568 to 26th January 1569 Mary Queen of Scots was imprisoned here. Besieged by the Parliamentarian forces in 1645, the castle capitulated, and was eventually dismantled. The N.E. tower fell in a storm in 1761, and in the early 19th century the S.W. tower and W. curtain were roofed. The castle, with square towers at the corners, and built round a rectangular courtyard, is one of the most interesting of its period.' The car park is at the west end of the village, just beyond the castle. Refreshments are served in the castle, which may be a factor in deciding whether or not to visit it at the beginning or the end of the walk.

Begin the walk by taking the road through the village and continue for three-quarters of a mile, passing the little dell of Apedale Beck, to the 'T' junction where the signpost reads 'Grinton 4½, Reeth 5½, Redmire ½'. Turn left uphill on the wide road; the road narrows and becomes much quieter beyond the quarry entrance. On to higher ground, you will see a short chimney – this is the old Cobscar smelt mill on Preston Moor. Apedale will shortly be visible on the left. Pass the first guide post, and leave the road at the second post half a mile further on, bearing left on to a stony track – the point at which those choosing to stroll into Apedale may leave the car.

The gradual descent into the valley reveals the shooting hut at Dent's Houses. Above and beyond are tracks leading to old mines where the spoil heaps are still to be seen but, having mellowed over the years, they are no longer a blot on the landscape. Up to the last century, the lead mining industry must have given Apedale a very different appearance from the quiet and remote scene now before us. The wide track snakes up the dale on the way to Crackpot in Swaledale; take it as far as you wish to go, before returning to cross tracks near the shooting hut.

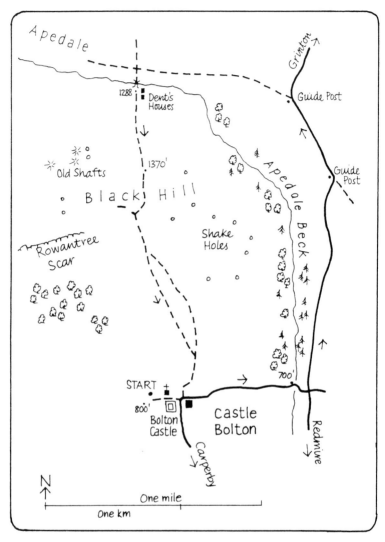

Circuit walkers now pass through a gate and over Apedale Beck on a bridge. This is National Park border country; from now on we are in the Park, having earlier been outside it. Pass the shooting hut, marked 'out of bounds', walking on a good green track by the side of a wire fence. Over to the left the chimney on Preston Moor can be seen again. On Black Hill go through a stile by the side of a gate across the road, where a whole new outlook emerges. Across Wensleydale, Penhill is prominent; the valley of Walden is to the right of it; Bishopdale goes away towards Wharfedale; and still further to the right is the distinctive shape of Addlebrough, seen over the stepped hills above Carperby – Wegber Scar and Great Wegber, rising to Woodhall Greets.

Descending, the scar seen on the immediate right is Rowantree Scar. A clear track leads to an enclosed farm lane – muddy in wet weather – and comes into the village 150 yards from the castle. In the wall at the junction a tap is conveniently placed for the benefit of the thirsty traveller.

Aysgarth Falls

*The hub of all Wensleydale is its most popular beauty spot –
Aysgarth Falls. Adequately signposted and properly provided with
car park, toilets, information centre and café, it may however be
thought hardly necessary to give it a chapter in this book. Some
people see only the upper falls and come away thinking they have
seen all there is to offer, missing the grandest of them all – the lower
falls. The following information is taken from the* Yorkshire Dales
National Park Guide *issued for the Countryside Commission; 'The
three sets of falls at Aysgarth are caused by the outcropping of hard
bands in the Yoredale Series and attract many visitors. The drop
allowed the construction of mills and the mill by the bridge (which
itself dates from 1539) is famous because it supplied the red flannel
for the shirts for Garibaldi's army.'*

USE the car park, which is on the Carperby side of the river. Walk
down the road to two notices on the left directing you to 'Middle
Force and Lower Force' and 'Keep to top footpath'. Follow this
for 100 yards and turn right for a sight of the middle force by
scrambling down the hillside on polished tree roots. This fall, which
is quite impressive, is often missed, especially in summertime when
the leaves are thick on the trees. Regain the footpath and pass
through a small iron swing gate, following the worn path as far as
a stile in the fence on the right, signposted to 'Lower Force'. From
the stile go straight down to a viewpoint of the falls, from which
you may first prefer to walk upstream to the top of the falls before
returning through the woods to a cleft leading down to the rock
floor at the water's edge. Here the clean rocks, beside rushing
water and beneath cliffs topped with trees, give the spot a holiday
atmosphere.

Return to the stile, from which you can simply go back the way
you came and walk along the road, first to the upper falls and then
by raised track to the car. Alternatively, you can complete the full
circuit by picking up the track signposted to Carperby which you
would have noticed earlier. The proper way to do this is to return
to the signpost and take a sharp right turn.

The track to Hollin House Farm is clearly marked by 'path' signs,
yellow arrows, white posts and stiles; the way through the farm yard
is also plainly indicated. Behind and across the Dale is Penhill; in
front, Bolton Castle comes into sight. Follow the farm road until a
'Footpath' notice is seen painted on the wall on the right beside a
tractor trail. Turn on this trail, following it 250 yards as far as a

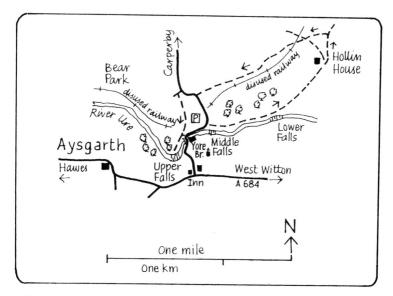

stile over the wall on the right. Do not go over it but turn squarely left to walk over grazing ground – marshy in parts – to a signpost by the side of the farm road. Follow the direction of the arm indicating Aysgarth, over a stile, to cut across the corner of a field to another stile. Cross the disused line and turn left, walking on the right of way which is just outside the old railway boundary.

Pass through a stile in the wall ahead and keep beside a wire fence on the left, a field away from the railway tracks. At the end of the field go through a gate on the left and walk towards the line, but turn right just before it, going through three fields to a gate into a wood. Twenty yards later turn right on a single track, then left, to continue in the line of march, going slightly uphill through trees and out on to the Carperby road by a stile at the side of a gate.

On the road turn right and, after a hundred yards, left through gates into Bear Park. Turn left immediately, passing to the right of a knoll and then bearing left to go through a gate in a wire fence. Continue downhill across a field to a stile in another wire fence, which leads to a path and an iron gate. Cross the old railway and turn left down steps to the car park – but the Upper Force is still to be visited. Take a Nature Trail track down to Yore Bridge and enter the grounds of Bear Park again by a wooden gate. Here it is pleasant to take in the beauty of the upper falls splashing over mossy rocks – not so dramatic as those already observed but the favourite of those who prefer the gentler scene. The view from the bridge is delightful but look out for traffic. Return to the car park by the footpath.

Askrigg's Waterfalls

To add to the simple enjoyment of beauty, some reference to the geology of Wensleydale, responsible for the creation of much of its splendour, is appropriate. Arthur Raistrick's chapter on 'Geology and Scenery' in the Yorkshire Dales National Park Guide *gives some helpful information. Writing about the Yoredale Series of limestone he says: 'The Yoredales are a series of thinner limestone occurring in rhythmic sequence with shale and sandstone, so that a "unit" of limestone, shale, sandstone, is repeated many times. The differing resistance to weathering of the limestone and shale is the cause of the terraces on the sides of Wensleydale and of the abundance of lovely waterfalls in all its stream-courses. The principal limestones, from the bottom upward, are Hardraw Scar, Simonstone, Middle and Main; these four are responsible for most of the obvious scars in Wensleydale. The repeated rhythmic units vary considerably in thickness and so give great variety to the scars . . . A section of the lower portion of the Yoredale Series is admirably displayed near Askrigg and in following this section you will see some fine waterfalls.*

ASKRIGG is the home of the authors, Marie Hartley and Joan Ingilby, whose book *Yorkshire Village* describes it in great detail. Park the car on the cobbles outside the stately parish church of St. Oswald and follow the road to the right of it, marked 'No through road. Footpath of Mill Gill Force'. Leave the houses on this narrow way, a gate across the road will soon be reached on which is a notice saying 'Private road'. On the right is a signpost 'Millgill Force' pointing to a trod across the field which leads to the north end of the charming complex of mill and farm buildings. Take this route and join a footpath beside the stream which is here known as Mill Gill Beck. Below, it it called Paddock Beck; in its higher reaches it has the name Whitfield Gill Beck.

Continue by the side of the stream as far as a finger post which points the way to Mill Gill Force across a substantial footbridge. Turn right after passing through a stile, keeping to the wall on the right and going through a series of stiles – in single file please. Soon you should hear the sound of a distant waterfall and if the trees are not in full leaf you should also see it; a stile in the wall on the right leads to another beside a finger post indicating Mill Gill Force. A good stony path leads down to the fall, and as you round a bend you will be impressed by its height – similar to that of Hardraw, from which the limestone takes its name, except that this is a broken fall. A fine pool is near the foot, and in the vegetation there are plenty of specimens for the botanist.

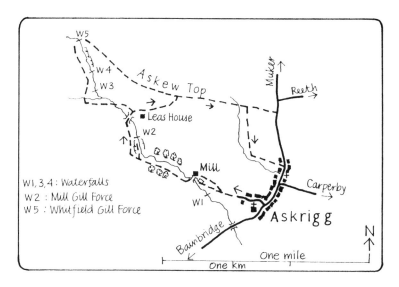

Return to the finger post and follow a waymarked path close to the stream. Across the dale on the left is Bainbridge, with the Roman fort to the left of it; behind the fort is Addlebrough; and rising steadily towards Wether Fell to the right of the village is the Roman road. After about a quarter-mile, turn right at a junction of paths and cross the bridge below Leas House. Bear to the left of Leas House, sloping upwards to join a bridleway which leads to a gate and the farm drive, continuing to the junction with the enclosed road along Askew Top.

To extend the walk half a mile each way, turn left up the road. At the end of it is a gate, just beyond which is a 'V' stile in the wall on the left to a path which gives views of the impressive Whitfield Gill Force. But there is no right of way beyond the gate. Return to Leas House drive end and continue down the lane along the basic route.

All walkers will certainly enjoy the straightforward walking down this lane, giving an opportunity to take in details of the Wensleydale scene ahead, with Penhill in the background. To the left front are the 'steps' of the hills seen from the other side in Walk 9, an interesting exercise being to identify the Yoredale Series. Cross a water splash, either through the water or over a footbridge. About 120 yards beyond is a large ash tree on the right. Go through a stile immediately past it and walk in the field on the left of a wall and a barn 50 yards from the tree. With the church tower in sight ahead, pass to the right of an attractive dry valley and leave the field where it narrows to the neck and a gate opening. The stream already

crossed in the lane will be seen ahead but do not cross it again –
bear left and walk beside it on a cart track to a stile and a gate,
keeping near the stream all the way to the village. Turn right
on the tarmac road so as to explore Askrigg on the way back to
the church.

Wether Fell and Bardale

Some fine walking country lies to the south of the river Ure between Bishopdale and Widdale. Semerwater is in the middle of the region, overlooked by Addlebrough, of distinctive shape.

TAKE the car to Bainbridge, well kept round a village green and famous for its hornblower and its Roman fort on Brough Hill – a drumlin. Motor to Marsett (3½ miles) via Countersett and Semerwater, leaving the car on the grass by the stream in the village. Return to the first lane immediately on the left, where there should be a public footpath sign although this was damaged when last visited.

Follow the gated farm road, turning left at the end through the gate leading to the farm 'Bella or Knight Close'. But instead of going down to the farm, keep to the wall on your right and go through a wicket gate in it. Go uphill half left to a stile about mid way in the cross wall. Go over it and continue in the same direction to a stile in another crossing wall. Keeping in the line of march, the crossing of the stream on the left is at the top end of a steep-sided cutting, soon after which will be seen a stile in the next wall. On the other side cross the field to a gap in the wall ahead and then diagonally to a stile near the corner of the field, which is a few yards to the right of a gap in the adjoining wall on the left. Over the stile, bear left uphill to pick up a double track bearing half left.

The Roman road, between walls, is now in sight. Join it at a metal gate and turn left. This is a good stony, grassy road, ideal for walkers. Looking back the track is typically Roman – long and straight – but ahead it curves upwards and round Wether Fell. The scene behind and to the left embraces Semerwater, Addlebrough beyond it, Penhill further away, and in good weather conditions the North York Moors on the other side of the Vale of Mowbray. Buckden Pike comes into sight on the left and as you reach the brow of the hill Penyghent is in front, slightly to the left of your line of march. The triangulation pillar, 2,015 feet, on Drumaldrace – the south-west tip of Wether Fell – is obscured on the immediate right by the curve of the hillside.

Join the hard road linking the heads of Wensleydale and Wharfedale, and turn left at the junction with the Cam End road (now tarred but not yet shown as such on the O.S. maps). At the first gate on the left, 200 yards further on, go through it to join a double green track downhill. Rounding two bends the path will be seen to

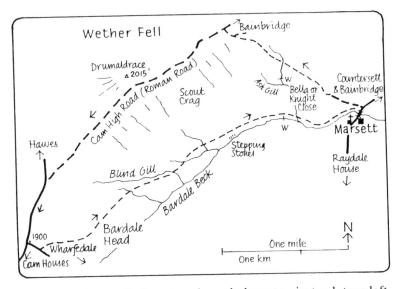

go to a gate in a wall; do not go through the gate – instead, turn left where a single path follows the wall down Bardale.

The rest of the route is simple. Keep to the wall on your right until you have passed a group of trees, but go through a gate in the wall before reaching a stone erection in the shape of the end of a Nissen hut – which was once almost certainly its function. On the other side of the wall make straight for Semerwater, which is almost always in view on this return journey. You are now on a green track on the brow of a small spur, passing through a series of gates and over streams, the second of which is Blind Gill, suitably named because it disappears into the ground below the crossing place.

The track brings you to stepping stones over Bardale Beck, but resist the temptation to go over to the other side where there is a well-defined route down the valley (a snare leading to boggy ground). Stay on this side – which has the added merit of carrying the right of way – and enjoy the delight of walking alongside the lovely Bardale Beck. Soon you will reach a waterfall and pool. Where better, and at what better time of day, to take a plunge? Below the pool and fall the stream bed is of solid limestone, falling into an impressive little gorge containing a succession of small waterfalls. The right of way is still on the left bank, but the right bank gives better local views and leads to a footpath to the village of Marsett and the car.

56

Semerwater and the Stake Pass

The attractions of the walk include one of Yorkshire's few lakes, about which Marie Hartley and Joan Ingilby say: "Semerwater has many charms and a traditional story. The legend of a city sunk beneath its waters has probably a basis in fact. Here were Iron Age lake dwellings, some of which may well have been submerged by a sudden flood. A causeway leads out into the lake from the strange rocks near the enormous limestone boulder of glacial origin called the Carlow Stone, and a Bronze Age spearhead was found some years ago on the north shore."

JUST outside Bainbridge, on the main road to Aysgarth, take the road to Stalling Busk – an uphill climb for 300 yards to a bend, beyond which park on the grass verge near a gate with a stile and a footpath finger post on the right. Follow the path uphill, roughly parallel to the valley of the Bain, England's shortest river, and pass to the left of an intake and building. Look back for a good view of the Roman camp on the top of the large drumlin outside Bainbridge. A single cattle trail skirts the hill ahead but keep up above it and climb over the top to a signpost in a crossing wall. Here are two stiles. Take the right-hand one and go forward over Bracken Hill. On the other side of the river is Bainbridge High Pasture, over which the Roman road takes its straight course to pass between Yorburgh, 1,686 feet, and Crag, 1,614 feet. Crag is the height rising above Semerwater which now comes into sight.

Go forward to a stile in a wall, another beside a tree and a gate in the wall beyond. Proceed downhill to a gate and stile quite close to a bend in the Bain. From this point, the path has been diverted in recent years and now follows the river all the way to Semerwater Bridge. Turn left on the road, pass the Carlow Stone near the lake side and keep on the road when it goes uphill, looking out for the sharp edge of Addlebrough ahead. Cross Little Ings Bridge, pass temporary buildings on the right and, opposite Low Blean Farm, go through the gate on the right at a footpath sign.

Now, with a wall between you and the lake, go through a succession of three stiles and on to a clear track above the water, well signposted, which rises and forks a quarter of a mile beyond the head of the lake. Keep left on the clearer path, through a stile and walk uphill on the left of a wall, on the other side of which is a ruined ivy-covered church. Go uphill, with a wall on the left and a stream on the right, entering a green lane and the village of Stalling

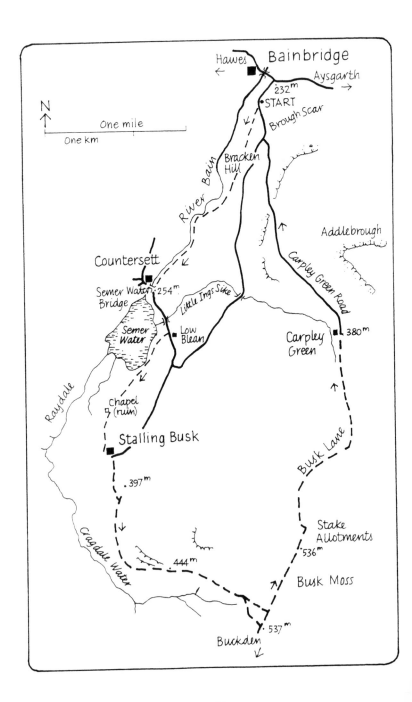

Busk. Pause to look across Raydale to the village of Marsett at the foot of Bardale, with Wether Fell behind (Walk 16).

In Stalling Busk, pass the church, phone box and posting box to arrive at a T-road. Here a decision must be made. We have now travelled a third of the distance of the full walk and there is an ascent to be made of about 700 feet. Should a return be made by going straight along the road on the left (and up the hill initially) back to the car, or by retracing steps?

Those doing the whole walk do turn left, but half-way up the hill take the turning on the right up a rough stony lane, soon to join the Stake Pass road with its better stony surface. Down on the right is Cragdale – the third of the three valleys at the head of the dale – and now there is to be a steady climb for 1½ miles on this famous Roman link between Bainbridge and Buckden in Wharfedale, fit for Land-Rovers but not for cars. Nearing the top, the road takes a sharp turn to the right, from which another acute turn (to the left) will be seen higher up. At the right-hand turn leave the road, go left through a gap in the wall, and keep straight on uphill on sheep tracks, with a wall on your left. Turn left at the first gate, joining a green track – between old walls – coming from the road.

Follow the green track over the open moor – Busk Moss – to pass through Stake Allotments. The track goes through a gate and now there is a good wall on the left and an old one on the right. Soon the route is downhill and Addlebrough is seen ahead and below, until, after a change of direction, it appears for a short time on the left. When it is again on your right front you will see a wall going away from you to the top of the hill. There is no right of way over it but this wall is sometimes used as a guide to the top from a track leading from the north of Carpley Green. Today our route is straight on through the farm of Carpley Green, after which the surface of the road is tarred. Semerwater comes into sight again on the left and the head of Wensleydale to the left front. Join the road from Stalling Busk; the car will soon be seen ahead.

Hardraw and Great Shunner Fell

No visit to Wensleydale would be complete without going to see England's highest waterfall above ground – Hardraw Force, a single drop of the waters of Fossdale Gill and Hearne Beck which join a mile up-stream. The waterfall is in an impressive gorge, noted for its acoustics, for here is the site of an old bandstand where brass band contests were held. To gain access, the public must pass through the bar of the Green Dragon Inn in the village where a small charge is made. A trip to the fall, if included in today's journey, would add a mile.

LEAVE the car at the west end of the village (spelt 'Hardrow' on O.S. maps, but rarely elsewhere, and surely never pronounced that way) just beyond the last building on the right which is a school. Here is a 'Pennine Way' signpost pointing to a narrow, enclosed roadway. Take this route as far as the gate leading to the open fell. Fifty yards from the gate the metalled Pennine Way bears to the left, but leave it and take the clear grassy track seen ahead. Looking back, the top of Ingleborough should soon be seen peeping over Snaizeholme Fell. The track is now the Hearne Coal Road – no longer used by miners – sometimes wide, sometimes a single path, depending on the terrain. It goes first towards a hump with a shooting house clearly seen, and then up the left-hand valley, keeping Hearne Beck down on the right. Encountering some boggy ground, the path peters out. It is as well to leave the right of way here to try to keep dry feet, and make towards what appears to be an overgrown spoil heap uphill on the left. Continue north-west over peat hags until the unmistakable Pennine Way is reached, liberally marked with cairns – useful guides through boggy ground. Turn right and make your way to the top of Shunner; on a fine day the summit cairn will have long been in sight.

The view from the top in good conditions is all-embracing. The Lake District mountains will already have been observed on the left on approaching the summit, as well as Wild Boar Fell and, behind it, the Howgill Fells. Looking back, the Three Peaks of Ingleborough, Whernside and Penyghent now show their full glory. Ahead, the fells at the head of Swaledale come into sight, such as Nine Standards Rigg behind Birkdale Tarn, High Seat and Hugh Seat a little nearer. For one of the best views down Swaledale itself, one must extend the walk further north on the Pennine Way to a slender beacon, adding half a mile each way.

The return journey keeps to the Pennine Way all the time, cairns

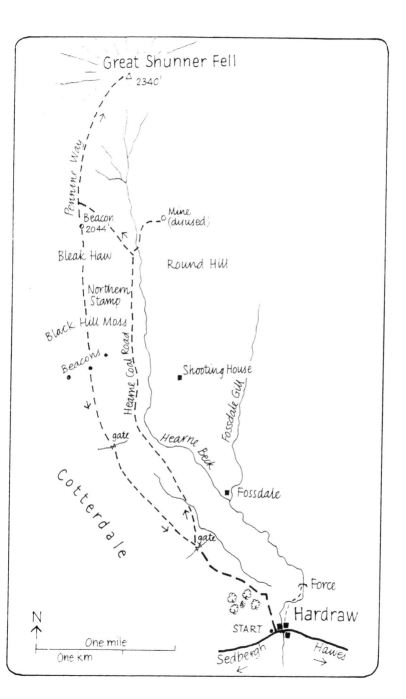

Great Shunner Fell
△ 2340'

Pennine Way

Mine (disused)

Beacon 2044'

Bleak Haw

Round Hill

Northern Stamp

Black Hill Moss

Hearne Coal Road

Beacons

Shooting House

Fossdale Gull

gate

Hearne Beck

Cotterdale

Fossdale

gate

Force

N

Hardraw

START

One mile
One Km

Sedbergh   Hawes

and a well-worn path making route finding simple. On the way down, a new feature is seen on arrival at a cairn nearly as big as the one at the top – Cotterdale is down on the right, looking peaceful. Many will regret the appearance of row upon row of conifers on Tarn Hill on the other side. The going becomes smoother as one joins another old coal road, coming in on the right from disused pits in Cotterdale, approaching the first of two gates below; between the gates, the sheep-cropped track is a delight. At the second gate the outward path is joined, steps being retraced through the lane.

Hell Gill

*Hell Gill, a dramatic gorge separating North Yorkshire and Cumbria,
marks the north-western boundary of Wensleydale. Hell Gill Beck
turns north, becoming the river Eden which empties into the Solway;
less than half a mile away is the river Ure, going south and east to
the Humber. In fact, splashes of rain on Ure Head, a mile upstream,
can fall inches from each other and take opposite directions on their
way to the sea.*

FROM the *Moorcock Inn*, which is on the Hawes/Sedbergh road,
take the road towards Kirkby Stephen for two miles, leaving the
car at Shaw Paddock before the road takes a sharp left turn under
the railway – the grass verge is wide enough. Walk straight forward
at the bend, passing through a gateway by the side of some sheep
pens on a good stone farm road. On rounding the corner, the first
of the fells of Mallerstang Common – the beautiful valley of the
upper Eden – comes into sight. This is Wild Boar Fell, a steep-
sided double 'table mountain'. Over the first bridge across the
river Ure, leave the farm road and go straight forward on a green
track to pass over the Ure for the last time on a small earth and
stone bridge. After bearing to the right uphill, the track goes over
well drained limestone land with scars in evidence on both sides.
The trees ahead are at Hell Gill bridge; the farm below the bridge
bears the same name. The track joined just before the bridge is the
High Way, an ancient trail from Hawes to Mallerstang, via Cotter
End, now used in part by the Y.H.A. for the annual 'Mallerstang
Marathon', a 25 mile walk from the old Garsdale Head Youth
Hostel embracing High Seat, Nine Standards Rigg, Tailbridge Hill,
Wild Boar Fell and Turner Hill.

Looking over the parapet of the bridge, you will be surprised to
see the depth of Hell Gill, with the water – almost hidden by vegetation – swirling down below. There is no right of way upstream,
and protection from the dangerous gorge is provided by a wall on
the right bank and a wire fence on the left, but it is worth encircling
these obstacles for a view of the stream tumbling into the gill. Here
among the bare, rippled, limestone slabs above a plunging pool,
one could establish a picnic place, from which one could wander
upstream at will, observing the beck bickering and tumbling, gain-
ing growth and strength, and acquiring character which deserves
more notability than it possesses in this remote part of the Pennines.

Return to the bridge, cross it again (assuming the Gill has been
encompassed in a clockwise direction) and go through the gate

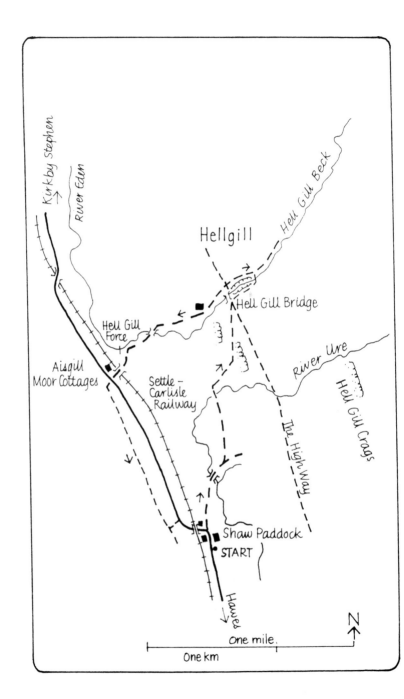

Kirkby Stephen →

River Eden

Hell Gill Beck

Hellgill

Hell Gill Bridge

Hell Gill Force

River Ure

Aisgill
Moor Cottages

Hell Gill Crags

Settle –
Carlisle
Railway

The Highway

Shaw Paddock
START

Hawes ↓

One mile

One km

N

64

immediately on the left. Pass the farm of Hell Gill, continuing on the farm road – with occasional diversions for more views of the Gill – and cross a wooden bridge. At a sharp left-hand bend, you should hear the sound of water falling. If you are not yet satisfied with so much beauty, go over to the fall, Hellgill force, 50 yards from the road, where you will find another Hardraw – not so high, but carrying more water, and a fine sight.

Soon you will come to a bridge over the railway. Pause and look back for a view of the fells of Mallerstang Edge – High Seat, three miles away; Hangingstone Scar, unmistakable and a little nearer; and Hugh Seat, behind it and along the line of an old wall forming the boundary of both the county and the National Park. The main road is reached at Aisgill Moor Cottages, where tea and coffee are advertised and a seat is provided opposite. Turning left, a three quarter mile walk along the road would bring you back to Shaw Paddock.

You could, however, avoid road walking by crossing to the other side, passing through a gateway and turning left. Keep to the right of a fence and then a wall, go through a gate in a cross wall and continue forward, keeping a wall on your left. Make for a gate in the wall ahead and beyond it, walk on a grassy track through reeds. At the brow of the hill look to the railway line on the left and see a bridge over the road – we shall eventually pass under it. Still keeping a field away from the road, on approaching the bridge observe a gate in the wall on the left. Leaving the right of way, go through the gate and down to the road through another gate. Some 200 yards of road walking brings you to the bridge. The car is round the bend on the other side of the railway line.

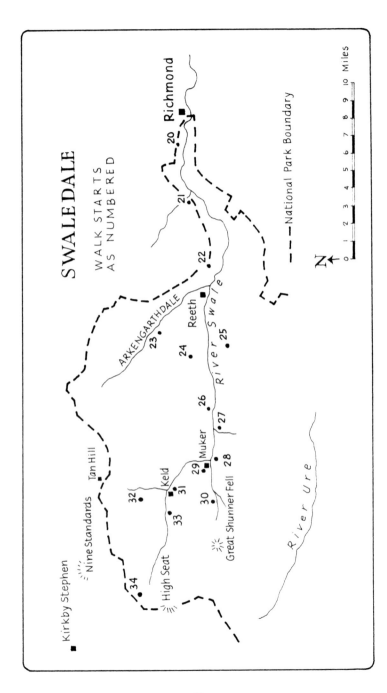

SWALEDALE

WALK STARTS
AS NUMBERED

Richmond

ARKENGARTHDALE

Reeth

River Swale

Muker

Keld

Tan Hill

Nine Standards

Kirkby Stephen

High Seat

Great Shunner Fell

River Ure

N

0 1 2 3 4 5 6 7 8 9 10 Miles

--- National Park Boundary

Swaledale

THE most dramatic approach to Swaledale for the motorist is over
the Buttertubs Pass from Hawes in Wensleydale. Pause at the fluted
pot holes by the road side – the Buttertubs themselves formed by
the action of water on limestone – and survey the picture. Lovely
Seat is to the east, across Cliff Gill; Great Shunner Fell to the west
– its top hidden by intervening ground. In front is Swaledale head,
divided into two parts by Kisdon, impressive in its isolation but
only 1,636 feet high, against Rogan's Seat's 2,203 feet, in the mass
behind it. Two miles further on brings one to Thwaite and an area
stretching from Muker and Gunnerside where, in high summer,
old-fashioned wild flowers still abound. In this respect it is similar
to the region of Hardraw and Hawes.

The dale does share other similarities with Wensleydale, but it is
much narrower and has only one side valley of size – Arkengarthdale; side streams are in gills, not big enough to be called dales. The
fells are not influenced to the same extent by the Yoredale Series of
limestones and are, therefore, not so much in terraces. On the other
hand, waterfalls occur in equal abundance. As with Wensleydale,
it is the walker of the Pennine Way who meets the finest downdale
prospect, this time from a beacon on Great Shunner Fell; the
motorist, however, may take in the scene in reverse from the
narrow road on Whitaside Moor between Askrigg and Healaugh.

So much for upper Swaledale. An introduction to the lower dale
is best effected by first visiting Richmond – a historic town of
beauty and character. Walk round the terrace below the castle
walls, then ride to Reeth through the wooded gorge. The colouring
of the trees in autumn sunlight must be seen to be believed. An
approach to the dale not so well known is along the straight tank
road to Halfpenny House, reached from Catterick village (on the
old Great North Road) or from Patrick Brompton, near Bedale. It
goes over Hauxwell and Barden Moors, handy for Catterick Camp.
Not only is the route a quick one, but it gives a comprehensive
view of Wensleydale and Swaledale together.

The high ground above both dales has been extensively mined
from Roman times. In Swaledale particularly (and Arkengarthdale)
lead mining has left its mark in the form of desert wastes, and
whereas the resultant scene on open moor may be one of desolation, the gills and gullies have often been enhanced by the scars
and shapes left by the excavations – enhanced, that is, for those
who love wild places. Those with imagination are able to visualise
the activities of the past – especially the 18th and 19th centuries.
The miners have left behind old roads and tracks of great worth
to present-day walkers. Good use has been made of many of them
in this book.

Upper Swaledale has long been a walker's paradise, vying in popularity with upper Wharfedale. The hospitality of the inhabitants is legendary. I have pleasant recollections of happy days between the wars based on the Muker home of Mr. and Mrs. David Harker, both, alas, now dead. Geoffrey Green, my walking companion on all the walks in this book – and very many others – knew their home even better. The hospitable traditions set by them, and hundreds more dalesfolk, still go on. May the reader enjoy – and have similar opportunities to remember – such happy days in so rich a setting.

Whitcliffe, Applegarth and Clapgate Gill

The area surrounding Richmond offers so many good walks that it is difficult to select the best representative one for this book. The ancient town itself deserves full exploration with its cobbled market place and streets – some of fine Georgian architecture, some older, solid and quaint. There is a small Georgian theatre, now quite famous. "The Lass of Richmond Hill" – Francis I'Anson – lived here, and the song was adopted by the Green Howards, reminding the listener that their regimental headquarters were at Richmond. Visit the castle and climb to the top of the keep for a well-rewarded small fee. A mile downstream – beyond Station Bridge – is Easby Abbey in peaceful and restful surroundings; it is reached by footpath past the old Grammar School, on this side of the river. Down below is the Swale, rushing and bubbling (a walk on the terrace below the castle walls shows the river at its best). At the foot of Bargate, to the west, is Richmond Bridge, upstream from which is the tree-clad, steep-sided, flat-bottomed dale – the course of the winding Swale. A delightful walk through the woods on the south side of the river starts on the right, immediately after crossing Richmond Bridge.

THIS walk is, however, to be on the north of the river. Motor out of the town on the main Reeth road, but before leaving the houses – where the main road turns sharply left (at Stockwell's corner) – go straight forward to the avenue of West Fields (an open public park is down on your left). Park the car by the road side where the tarmac finishes – between Whitcliffe and High Leases farms. A notice reads "No through road. Farm only".

Continue on foot past High Leases. On the left across the valley notice Hudswell and the outskirts of Catterick Camp. Go through a metal gate, passing a signpost "Private Woods. Please keep to the public path". The track crosses the top of a field before entering Whitcliffe Wood. Through the trees the river can be seen winding below; then a caravan site and on the skyline ahead, Hutton's Monument, beyond Marske. This is a popular walk on a broad, green, stony track. Emerging from the wood, over a stile, the track continues forward. On the right hand side, on the skyline, can be seen the monument to Willance's Leap – to be visited on the return.

We are now entering the district of Applegarth, the farm on the left being East Applegarth. Do not go down to it – go straight

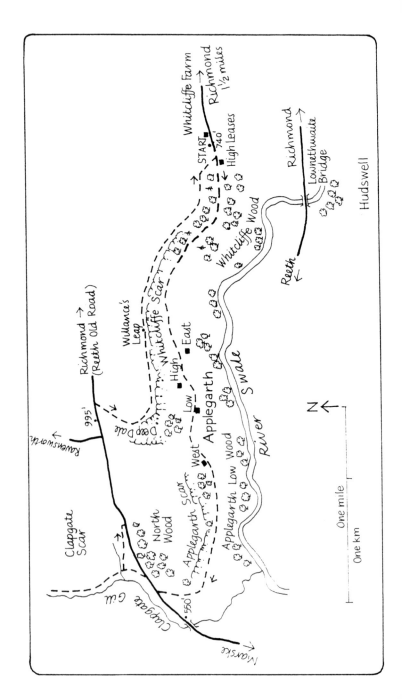

ahead on a green track, through a gateway or over a waymarked stile beside it, and to the right of some modern farm buildings, leaving the field through a gate at the far end and cross a tarmac road. Follow a marked footpath on the left of the road, first through a slit stile. Cross a field to a substantial stile beside a gate. Cross a road and continue in the line of march of a slit stile, also way-marked. Another stile takes you to a large pasture. Keep in the same direction to a stile. Cross a field and a small stream to a gate and to the left of West Applegarth farm and continue on the farm road, which curves to the right under Applegarth Scar.

The pastoral scene between here and Hutton's Monument enchants the eye. Clapgate Beck flows peacefully between fields. Up the valley, towards Clapgate Gill, the fields on the far hillside are terraced, indicating ancient cultivation; on higher ground, woodlands complete the local vista. Marske Hall can be seen, and beyond it the hills of middle Swaledale are in evidence. Across the dale, the rounded How Hill stands out well, although only 825 feet high, between it and Downholme Moor is the Leyburn road.

The farm road emerges on to the old Richmond to Reeth road. Turn right, and for an optional diversion of half a mile each way to a delectable picnic place in Clapgate Gill, pass through a gate on the left less than two hundred yards away. Follow a tractor trail, soon to turn downhill on a single track, and cross a small stream on stones – the main stream of Clapgate Gill is down on the left. Tracks lead through the Gill ahead as far as a cross wall where the right of way stops, the reason for which becomes clear on reading red warning signs: "Danger. Ministry of Defence range. Keep out while red flags or lamps are displayed". Just before the cross wall in the wall on the left is a small gate leading to the water side – a splendid place in which to loiter.

Return by the same route to the side stream, from which the right of way goes back to the road by way of the gate through which we passed earlier. Turn left and continue up the road, passing the junction to Whashton and Ravensworth. At a dip in the road turn right over a cattle grid beside a notice: "Private road. East and Low Applegarth. Footpath only". Almost immediately turn left off the farm road on to a green track and walk beside a wall on the lip of Deep Dale. In good weather the hills of Wensleydale can be seen over the Swaledale hills, Penhill being particularly prominent. The well-named Deep Dale opens out and we come to the balancing stone seen from below, now observed to be on a man-made wall or kiln.

Now it is pleasant to walk alongside the wall which is above the cliffs of Swaledale, passing above clefts containing junipers and fallen rocks, with no danger to careful walkers. Lower Swaledale and the outward route are seen below. Soon two monuments are reached, erected to the memory of William Willance's leap in 1606 when his horse fell down the cliff but his own life was "miraculously" saved. Continuing between the boundary wall and the steep slope, a point is reached where Lownethwaite Bridge may be seen below. Here cross a stile to walk on the field side of the fence. Eastwards the view is magnificent – across the Vale of Mowbray are the Hambleton and Cleveland hills, and to the south more Pennine hills have come into sight. Breasting the brow of the hill, the keep and towers of Richmond are in view. Go down the hill to rejoin the farm road at High Leases, and turn left for the starting point near Whitcliffe farm.

Marske Beck

This walk is suitable for most people, being on good surfaces and using comparatively easy gradients. Marske is a lovely, well-kept village, lying in delightful surroundings. Beautiful trees, clipped hedges, formal gardens and cared-for properties combine to delight the eye. Marske Hall, now in flats, was the home of the Hutton family, two members of which became archbishops. On a hill to the south-west is an obelisk known as Hutton's Monument, the grave of Matthew Hutton (1814). Marske Beck flows through a fine valley, not big enough to be called a dale in its own right but having all Swaledale's attributes in miniature. Scoured by the rushing overflow waters from the melting Stainmore Glacier, some ten to thirty-thousand years ago, it is narrowly confined between a limestone edge above Limekiln Wood and the steep Telfit Bank which we shall pass below on the outward journey and above on the return.

THE car may be left on the west side of Marske bridge without giving cause for annoyance to householders, most of whom are on the other side of the beck. Walk across to the east side taking the left-hand of two stiles – the one which leads to steps down to the stream. After only about a hundred yards of stream-side walking, go through a gate on the right into a field, through which take a diagonal course upwards towards the fourth telegraph pole. Join a narrow metalled road at a cattle grid, underneath the crag on Marske Edge.

Continuing up the valley, pass a group of smart cottages, a Methodist church and some notable stables – on the site of the former Clints Hall, now pulled down. After passing another well-kept house, the rough road enters Clints Wood, soon emerging to reveal the limestone edge to the right front. The path divides: take the left fork, pass through a gate and keep straight on. A notice on this gate reads "Out of Bounds" but do not be deterred, it is to troops who have a training ground nearby. There is a right of way to the public on the bridleway ahead. Before reaching the farm ahead – Orgate – turn down to join a concrete farm road to the stream which may be crossed either on a metal footbridge or a concrete cattle bridge. Choose the latter for a sight of Orgate Force, upstream, a wide waterfall especially impressive after rain.

Join the valley road at some new all-purpose farm buildings. Go straight ahead on the road, and then follow the path which cuts across the fields on your right to arrive at Telfit Farm. On reaching the brow of the hill, leave the road which turns sharply left and go

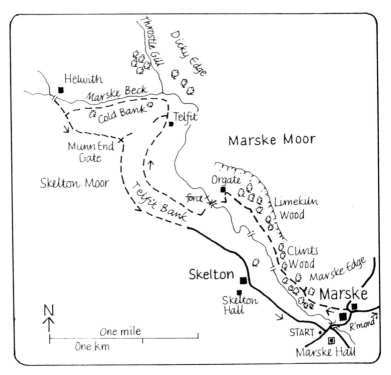

through a gate in the wall ahead (the right of way here is the subject of a diversion order which will be signposted). Go down the hill on cattle tracks over bumpy ground in the direction of Throstle Gill which can be seen ahead. Near the junction of Throstle Beck with Marske Beck go through a gate in the wall on the left.

On the other side of the gate is a green path through a secluded, serene, steep-sided glade. Eventually, the buildings of Helwith are in sight on the other side of the beck; the path takes one gradually uphill towards a gate in a far cross wall, but before reaching the distant gate pass through a gap in a broken wall and turn left on a green, stony track coming up from the ford and footbridge below Helwith. The engineered gradient indicates association with lead mining of former centuries. Pause half-way up the hill to look back beyond Helwith to the wooded valley occupied by Holgate Beck which springs from Moresdale Gill in New Forest. It is a pleasing sight.

The track passes through a wall at Munn End Gate and goes over the end of Skelton Moor to the top of Telfit Bank from which there is a fine ridge route home, giving views of the early part of the journey and lower Swaledale beyond. All the time Hutton's

74

Monument is ahead. Passing through a gate, the path continues gradually downhill with a wall on the right; now in an enclosed lane, it is green at first, becoming stony as it steepens. Join a tarmac road and pass through Skelton, the Hall now being partly converted into cottages. At the next junction turn left for Marske bridge.

Marrick Priory and Fremington Edge

*Walks beside the river Swale abound in the Reeth/Grinton area.
The route now to be described could be joined from Grinton by
taking the riverside path from the north end of the bridge, returning
by road from High Fremington, adding about half a mile to the
journey. Otherwise, the car could be parked at the Marrick Priory
junction with the old Richmond road near Low Fremington, or
400 yards along this single track road, near the river. Continue
on foot to Marrick Priory, formerly a house for Benedictine nuns,
now used as a residential youth centre. Casual visitors are made
welcome.*

LESS than a hundred yards past the Priory, turn on to a green track
upwards towards a gate, through which enter a wood. Immediately
you are on the nuns' stone stairs or nuns' causey. The stones all the
way through the wood are particularly useful in or after wet weather
when the overflow of a stream makes good use of the indentations
of the feet of centuries. At the top of the wood, turn round on
reaching a gate and stile for a fine view of the Priory and the valley
beyond. A long sweep of the Swale is seen below.

The track, now green, continues upwards by the side of the wall
you have been following through the wood, crosses a field to a
muddy enclosure by a barn – look for a grand prospect of lower
Swaledale from here – and enters a lane to pass a chapel on the left
and a disused church on the right. It reaches the village of Marrick
at a road junction at which a signpost says "Public Footpath to
Marrick Priory", which also indicates the route of Wainwright's
Coast to Coast walk.

Turn left, leaving the village on a narrow tarmac road. Such a
surface gives one the opportunity to survey the landscape on the
move. Soon, on the right, the Hutton monument comes into sight
– erected to the memory of one of the family who lived at Marske
Hall – then further to the east two masts near Richmond, near the
start of Walk 20. Between the monuments and the masts is the
valley of Marske Beck, in the area of Walk 21. The people in the
farm house on the right – Nun Cote Nook – must be ideally situated
for extensive views of lower Swaledale. The stream in the valley
beyond the farm house bears four names all within two miles:
Dales Beck, Ellers Beck, North Gill and Oxque Gill. No prizes are
offered for the pronunciation of the last name! Before reaching the
T-road, Swaledale, with Great Shunner Fell at its head, comes into
sight over the wall on the left.

76

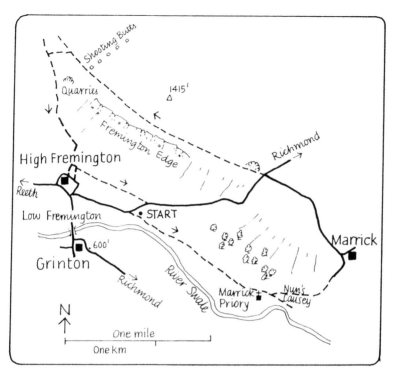

The T-road is the old main road from Richmond to Reeth. Cross it and go through the left hand of two gates, or the narrow slit stile in the wall at the side of it. Go up to the gate ahead which takes you to the right-hand side of the wall going away in front of you – this wall will be with you for the next mile-and-a-half. On sheep-cropped grass, look back for views of the Cleveland and Hambleton Hills and look across Swaledale for the roads out of Grinton for Redmire and Leyburn. The track passes from green turf to heather, leaving the wall slightly and rejoining it near the brow of the hill. Looking over the wall from time to time, first Grinton and Grinton Bridge appear and then Reeth momentarily. All the time up the Dale, Feetham and Low Row villages are in sight. Calver Hill comes into view, shapely and inviting to be climbed, and, rounding a slight bend, you will see Arkengarthdale with Fremington Edge straight ahead.

Still on the right of the wall, pass over some lead mining waste and climb a wooden stile over a cross wall – 300 yards beyond it, our left-hand wall deteriorates and is no longer surmounted by barbed wire. Go through the first gap, cut diagonally forward across to the cliff top and pick up tracks sloping downhill to join

77

the quarry road – stony and cropped grass – descending to the left. Reeth is now to the right and Arkengarthdale behind.

Keep to the main track into the valley. Soon after it becomes enclosed by walls turn left at the first fork. High Fremington and Grinton are straight ahead, but to return to the car through fields take the first narrow lane on the left – indicated by a "Public Footpath" sign. The lane soon turns to the right, but leave it here to pass through a stile straight on. Cross a field to the gate and another lane; then cross the lane, pass through a gate, a field and another gate in the line of march. Continue forward, now with a wall on your right and through another gate, the wall this time being on your left. Pass through first a stile in a cross wall and then one in a rebate in the wall on your left; keep in the same direction across the final field to a public footpath sign and the last stile, arriving again at the old Richmond road. Turn right for the car at the corner 200 yards away, or down the road on the left by the riverside.

Arkengarthdale and Slei Gill

Reeth, fully provided with hotel and bed and breakfast accom-
modation – and a Youth Hostel at nearby Grinton – makes an ideal
walking centre. Many rights of way enable the visitor to enjoy the
riverside, gills and moorland, often on old tracks from mining days,
not only in Swaledale but also in Arkengarthdale.

MOTORING from Reeth, a pause on Reeth Low Moor is reward-
ing. Wide verges allow the driver to pull off the road at popular
picnic places. Calver Hill is on the immediate left: Arkengarthdale
stretches away in front of you. Fremington Edge is across the
valley – we shall later be walking to the north of it – and below us
are the twin villages of Arkle Town and Langthwaite. Take your
fill of the prospect before you; then continue to Arkengarthdale
Post Office in Langthwaite, park the car on the wide verge nearby
and walk down to the bridge over Arkle Beck. After admiring
the quaint village, turn right to follow the beck downstream on
a cart road.

The best time for this walk is after rain when the becks are full;
now, when the Arkle will be rushing and tumbling by your side,
and later, when the waterfalls in Slei Gill will be at their best.
Passing a strong metal bridge coming in from Arkle Town, the
road immediately turns towards the trees on the left, under which
it keeps a course parallel to the stream, one field away.

Now in a delightful woodland walk, the path takes a left fork,
leaves the trees to go up-valley, and then takes a right-hand turn to
Storthwaite Hill on the other side of Slei Gill. But leave the track
at this right turn and go straight forward through a gap in a wall,
adjacent to a barn. The intention now is to go up the gill on old
mine tracks, keeping fairly close to the stream until it is joined – at
a corner – near the top. On the way, cross some boggy land on
stones, pass old mines and notice a cairn across the valley, marking
Fell End which is at the north-west end of Fremington Edge. After
climbing a stile over a barbed wire fence, observe mining desolation
ahead; but as the valley narrows fine waterfalls and ledges in the
stream bed lend enchantment to the scene. The track reaches the
water's edge when the valley narrows; turn the corner for the sight
of another noble fall and the head of the gill, where there is more
evidence of mining.

Arriving at a gate in a cross wall, notice an old kiln at the junction
of two streams. Tracks go below and to the left of it, the left-hand
(upper) track being recommended. Cross the side stream where it

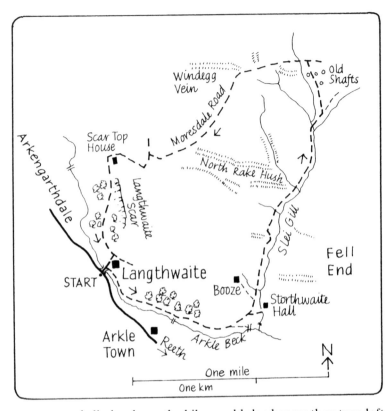

narrows and climbs above the kiln on old slag heaps; then turn left on a single track through heather and later through bracken. The right of way is shown to follow the main stream on the right, but the track we are on cuts off a triangle, passing some old pit shafts, now appearing as hollowed-out hills. A subsidiary stream is on the left. Join a tractor trail beyond the old pits, upwards through bracken, and within half a mile take a left turn on a stony, grassy, moorland road. We are now just below the Moresdale Ridge on Booze Moor, the track being known as the Moresdale road. Follow it, ignoring side turnings, to kilns and old workings at the top of the moor, continuing – now downhill – as far as the moor edge where the road takes a sharp right turn. Pause to look at what is now revealed. Arkengarthdale is before you; down on the right is the Stang road to Barnard Castle – the structure around a cattle grid, painted white, identifies it.

Leave the road here and turn left on to a Land Rover track, following it for about 250 yards where a wall on the right descends into a cleft. Go down to a small gate and continue down the gully;

when emerging on to the cropped grass of the fell side, you should see below another small gate near the right-hand end of a wood and to the left of a sheep fold. Continue down to the gate, turn left, and step out on a green bridleway on the other side of the wall.

Pass through a gate to the right of Scar Top House, now un-occupied, and follow the track gradually downhill to a small wooden gate near the wood edge. Continue in the same direction through the wood, first with a wire fence on the right, then between walls below Langthwaite Scar and on a track through the wood, first with a wire fence on the right, then between walls below Langthwaite Scar and on a track through the open wood until the bottom edge is reached. From here you should see the white-painted C.B. Hotel, then the church and village of Langthwaite. Continue just within the wood as far as a steep, narrow tarmac road (Langthwaite to Booze) and then turn right. You are back in Langthwaite in no time.

Hard Level Gill and Great Pinseat

This is another walk to appeal to those who love wild places and, with imagination, can picture the lead mining activities of former centuries. Surrender Bridge may be reached by car from Healaugh, Feetham, or Langthwaite in Arkengarthdale. The roads are tarmac but narrow, and there are steep hills to contend with on the Feetham and Langthwaite roads. Assuming the Healaugh road is chosen, take the road signposted to Kearton at the top end of the village for two miles of lovely views up Swaledale on the left and Calver Hill on the right. The well-known bridge is at the junction of several ancient routes. Park the car by the side of the beck, which changes its name every mile or so (lower down it is Barney Beck).

TAKE the track up-stream on the east side, marked by a notice saying "Public Bridleway". It is stony with cropped-grass verges, capable of taking lorries to a quarry up the gill. The swift but winding stream below has banks of stone waste. The road descends to ruined industrial buildings at stream level; keep straight on, to the right of the beck and past a working quarry. Climb up-hill to a cattle grid, passing Level House Bridge down on your left – it leads to the famous disused Old Gang lead mines. Keep straight on, with the stream on your left, now known as Flincher Gill.

The path crosses the stream and bears right to pass to the left of an old *level*. It crosses the stream again, passes through a gate, bears right up the hill and becomes stony and less obvious before winding round some old spoil heaps. You will see on your left a stone wall, to be joined later, but keep on the track and make for a heap of stones on top of the highest spoil heap. Turn left before reaching this cairn, and leave the right of way, stepping over heather to the wall. Walk along the wall side to the triangulation pillar on the other side, 1,914 feet above sea level. Go through a gap in the wall and admire the view of Arkengarthdale below. The narrow, tarred road on the other side of the dale is the Stang road to Barnard Castle. Whaw is in the valley, to the left of it.

Since the first edition of this book was written, the wall near the triangulation pillar has been rebuilt and it may prove to be too much of an obstacle. If so, return to the right of way where it passes through the highest spoil heap and continues on the track which turns south-east from the old mines to take a course roughly parallel to Bleaberry Gill about 500 yards from the stream. This track goes on for two miles from the mines, joining the Langthwaite/Healaugh road. Turn right for the car little more than half a mile along the road.

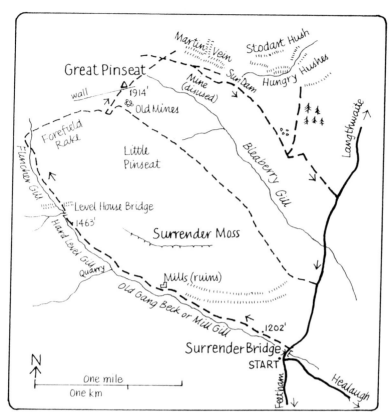

For those continuing on the original route from the trig point there is more heather to cross – to reach the moor edge in direct line beyond a prominent spoil heap. Fix your eye on some shorter grass at the lip; you could avoid some heather-hopping by using tracks parallel to the wall for about 400 yards, but turn left off these tracks before reaching a wooden hut. Cross some marshy ground to reach the crest and look for a faint double track going right. Join some old mine workings and bear right to go beside a series of spoil heaps, keeping Arkengarthdale in sight on your left.

Another diversion from rights of way is now suggested in order to visit the *hushes* on the left, slightly downhill. Exploration is in the hands – or the feet – of the reader, but one suggestion is to see the remains of the Sun Dam, now disused, in a little valley. Cross the top of the ravine on a sheep track leading to Hungry Hushes, explore at will and then make your way up-hill to join a well-defined unclassified road. Turn left, keeping to the track as far as a mining complex where the road sweeps to the right to rejoin the right of way. Turn left, and left again, past the mine to go steeply downhill by the line of some shooting butts. Bouldershaw House is seen below and you are now looking straight down Arkengarthdale.

At the hard road, turn right. It is now a matter of continuing along the road to the car but on the way you will come down to the attractive Bleaberry Gill at Fore Gill Gate. Here is a picnic area, obviously very popular, where the road crosses the beck on a ford – but a foot-bridge is provided. Continuing along the road brings one back to the point of departure.

Whitaside Moor and Apedale Head

This excursion affords an opportunity to observe some of the best and most varied of Swaledale's scenery. On one memorable winter's afternoon, when the author and writer of the foreword of this book were in the area, there was a covering of snow on the high ground. Shafts of sunlight picked out Fremington Edge, and pink rimmed clouds gave a fine background to Calver Hill, white and stark. Below, the Swale flowed darkly and the black gash of Gunnerside Gill contrasted with the white hills. Dominating the background was Great Shunner Fell, its top cairn visible at first but soon to be lost behind the nearer Crackpot Moor, topped with a cairn at Blea Barf, 1,772 feet above sea level. Occasional wisps of slow-moving low cloud gradually changed the scene, as did the light from the lowering sun towards the end of the day.

MOTORING to the starting point, take the narrow road to Askrigg a mile up the Dale from Healaugh. Climb steadily for a mile-and-a-half until reaching a gate on the left of a sharp bend in the road (when passing an old quarry on the left where a few cars could be parked, there is about a quarter-of-a-mile to go – stop at the first gate on the left). Park on the grass verge and continue up-hill, now on your feet. Alternatively, you may prefer to leave the car further along the road on the open moor.

On the road, cross over two gills and notice a private garage on the left. Turn left off the road on a double stony track just beyond, at first in the direction of a shooting box near the hill top, but soon turning sharply to the left. The track crosses the stream – Crag Sike – and continues alongside it to go through some swampy ground and past some old mines. Cross a stream and pass two heaps of stones on mounds – from here you can see another cairn on the skyline. Pass two more cairns on the way to it; 50 feet before it, turn right and when reaching a gully turn left, to go through a gate in the parish boundary double fence. While you are here, have a look at the round shaft of an old coal mine. It is dangerous but fenced – if you throw a stone down, you will find it is deep. If you wish to continue into Apedale (Wensleydale), take the track to the left beyond the shaft. Otherwise retrace your steps as far as the double cairn, half a mile away.

Continue down the track to a prominent heap of large stones, from which turn off to cross the heather to the right. A right of way exists here but it is difficult to find a path; soon however, you will reach the steepish side of Birks Gill. Cross the water and make for

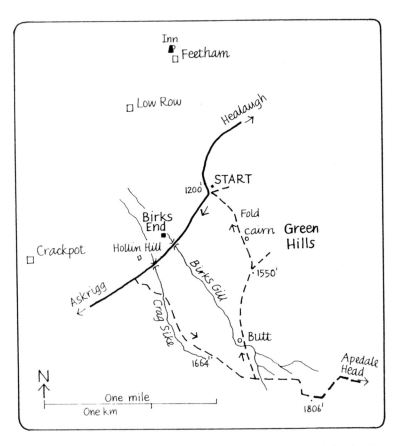

the shooting butt labelled No 6, picking up a single track in the line of march, but losing height and making for the rough end of Green Hills. An obvious track continues along the top but find your way down to the left on reaching the edge.

In good visibility the hotel at Feetham will be seen on the other side of the Swale. In line with it, at the foot of the scarp, a dark tall cairn should be discerned. Go quickly down, making for the cairn (not to be confused with another cairn which comes into sight on the right at the top of the nab) and pick up sheep tracks continuing towards the hotel. Pass a sheep fold, through a gate and take a half-left turn in the field to a gate leading to the road and the car.

86

Gunnerside Gill

The long history of lead mining in Swaledale has been set out in detail in several books. No better example of the remains of mines can be found than in Gunnerside Gill. Mining has retained – even enhanced – in the gills a certain stark and grim beauty, especially for those enchanted by wild places. But on the moors between the gills there is desolation in deserts of stone.

IN Gunnerside, find the notice "Public path to Gunnerside Gill" on the east side of the bridge across the road from the Kings Head Inn – the car may be parked on the other side of the stream – and walk up the wide track beside tumbling water. Just before reaching the old school buildings, turn up the narrow lane on the right, then resume progress up the valley. The path passes through woodland above stream level and reaches some old workings almost at the side of the stream. Over a stile in a wire fence, go up hill to the side of a wall, keeping it on your right and, later, a barbed wire fence on your left, going over a stile where they meet. Keep to the track up-hill from the stream by the side of a wall, pass some spoil heaps and, opposite a ruined building, go over a stile in the wall. The track then slopes upwards, passes to the right of a wall and levels out; leaving the wall, continue up-hill and up-valley on a broad track to cross two little streams in quick succession.

Opposite is Botcher Gill in which waterfalls help to make an attractive picture. Pass below the great blocks of stone making up Swine Bank Scar – at a junction with another track below the scar, the single path ahead may be clearly seen. The scene is fascinating, even though wild, grim and desolate; hushes come into sight with ruined buildings below them and on the other side of the valley. Nevertheless, this is great walking country, with springy turf beneath the feet. Soon we meet Wainwright's *Coast to Coast Walk*, which comes down the gill and goes up to the right – up Bunton Hush.

Pass to the right of ruined buildings, taking the track forward and upward; at Friarfield Hush we are opposite the impressive North Hush – also on the other side of the gill can be seen the sloping road to be taken on return. Think of the lives led by the thousands of miners in the past – chiefly in the eighteenth and nineteenth centuries; probably walking to work in the black hours, morning and night, often wet through; tunnelling in equally dark and possibly wet conditions through their working hours. Picture carts on the roads seen about you, heavily laden with lead ore,

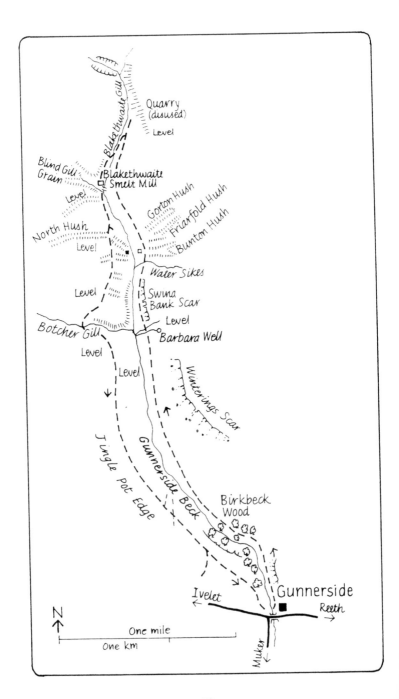

Blakethwaite Gill

Quarry (disused)

Level

Blind Gill Grain

Blakethwaite Smelt Mill

Level

Gorton Hush

Friarfold Hush

North Hush

Level

Bunton Hush

Water Sikes

Level

Swina Bank Scar

Level

Botcher Gill

Level

Barbara Well

Level

Winterings Scar

Level

Jingle Pot Edge

Gunnerside Beck

Birkbeck Wood

Ivelet

Gunnerside

Reeth

Muker

N

One mile

One km

toiling up the slopes. Look below to the Blakethwaite Smelt Mill, seen at the junction of Blakethwaite Gill and Blind Gill (which together form Gunnerside Gill). See the course of the flue in the cliff behind it, reaching the base of a stumpy chimney some 150 feet above the furnaces. Dr. Raistrick tells us that in this flue much of the lead fume was condensed and so saved.

You could descend here for a good stream crossing and an early return. But, for nearer views of Blakethwaite Gill, continue on the good turf track, between heather and stone; observe a fine waterfall near the next ruined building and explore up-stream as much as you will, along the gorge, beneath the cliffs. Returning, find the best crossing of the beck – which should not be difficult unless it is in spate. In any case there is a good bridge to cross at Blakethwaite Smelt Mill, but cross earlier if you can for good views of the water-fall. On the west side a single track goes down to the smelt mill, which merits exploration. In one chamber, the cast iron columns remain in the furnace house. The building nearby, with a fine arch still standing, was the peat store which kept a year's supply of fuel for the furnaces. The high-level, single slab bridge between the buildings is unique. The flue in the cliff may now be examined more closely.

Stride across the water of Blind Gill Grain – a look at the map will show that higher up it has travelled a considerable distance underground – and step out on the miner's track, green now but probably not when it carried tons of lead in years past. Keep to the main track, passing through North Hush on a raised road. Join a wide track which contours round Botcher Gill. Go through a gate and keep stepping out until the road takes a distinct turn to the right; leave it here, striking off to the left across open moor towards Gunnerside Bridge, which should be seen across Swaledale. Some-times a track will be found, sometimes not, but head towards the lip of Gunnerside Gill to reach a line of hawthorns. Continue down the hill into a gully to a stile on the left of three renovated houses in Gunnerside. The stile is opposite Barclays Bank by the side of the car park.

Ivelet Bridge and Oxnop Gill

On National Park notice boards displayed, with maps, in Muker and Gunnerside appears: "Ivelet Bridge. This fine single span bridge lying just aside from the Gunnerside/Muker road is the reputed haunt of a headless dog whose appearance is locally regarded as an ill omen. More factual is the coffin stone at the north end of the bridge, at which, in former times, weary mourners would rest their burden, while treading the Corpse Way between Muker and Grinton church in the days when Grinton church had to serve the whole of Upper Swaledale."

NOT only is the bridge itself worth a visit – do not attempt to go over it in a low slung car – but its setting also is very fine, over rippling river and beside towering trees. Park under the trees and, after admiring the bridge, set off up the steep road alongside the cascading Oxnop Beck. Turn right on the main road and, after less than 200 yards, turn left through a gate opposite a barn. Go uphill through the field, keeping near the beck and observing the water-falls. Go over a stile in the wire fence ahead and follow a yellow waymarked route which keeps above the line of the private woods. At a yellow-topped isolated post look back for a good view of Gunnerside and Swaledale. Oxnop Hall is down on the right as you continue on the footpath. Marie Hartley and Joan Ingilby tell us that here lived George Kearton, a rumbustious figure, who followed hounds in a pony chaise when he was 100, and who died aged 125 in 1764. The house has mullioned windows with ornamental dripstones.

Keep above the trees, skirt meadowland in single file and leave it over a stile in the corner. Continue with a short wall on your left and at the corner where the wall turns away, follow the direction of a yellow arrow across the middle of a rough field, rising to a metal gate beside which on the wall are yellow patches. On the other side is the Askrigg road. Turn left on it and pass a farm building on the other side of a narrow field on the left. Go through the next gate into the field and continue forward diagonally across it. Stride across a stream and turn left to pass through a gap in the wall beside the stream. Go through the next gate in the wall on the right, or a stile beside it, and cross the next field diagonally to a cattle crossing in Stony Gill. Go through a gate in the wall on your right front, turn left and with this wall on your left go to the top end of the field, leaving it through a gap in the same wall near a barn in the next field. Turn right to a gate in the corner of the barn field. Below is Oxnop Gill, with a footbridge over the beck.

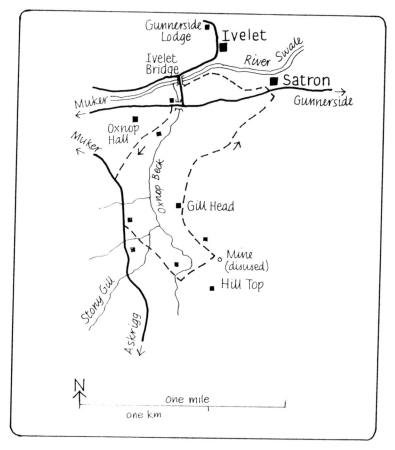

Ascend the wide track leading up the other side but do not go as far as the barn round the corner; instead, keep to a clear track beside some barbed wire fencing, above trees, about fifty feet from the beck. On reaching the wall on the right, continue forward to drop down into a depression and go through a stile in the wall on the left. One is in the area of a disused mine, now overgrown but much in evidence. Cross the little valley, bearing left to a small gate in a wall below a barn. The Askrigg road is now seen across the Gill, with Oxnop Side rising above it.

Cross a paddock to a stile. On the other side keep to the right of the wall going forward; this takes you to a stile in the wall on the right. Turn left on the other side, joining a track bearing right on the right-hand side of a wall, and pass to the right of Gill Head Farm to join a tarmac road going downhill. On the other side of

Swaledale is Gunnerside Lodge, above the hamlet of Ivelet, the shooting lodge belonging to Lord Peel. Many are the disadvantages of walking on hard roads – but this is narrow and the verges are good to walk upon. An advantage is that one may lift one's eyes from one's feet and take in the beauties of the countryside. Here one can see at a single sweep Muker, Satron and Gunnerside; the Swale; and the course of the Corpse Way, of macabre memory but lasting attraction.

Arriving at the main road in the hamlet of Satron, cross it to a "ginnell" immediately opposite, at the bottom end of which are two stiles on the left leading to a paved trod through the field. Follow this path as far as two adjoining stiles, crossing the right-hand one and going diagonally through the next field on a clear single track towards the Swale, soon to be seen flowing quietly below. Bear left for a riverside walk back to Ivelet Bridge, seeing through trees its exquisite proportions and beauty of line.

Thwaite and Muker

It is pleasant to walk beside the stream between Thwaite and Muker – known first as Thwaite Beck and then Muker Beck. Ancient footpaths link these two delightful villages, and we shall follow them in this walk. To make a circuit keeping road walking to the minimum, tracks on Muker Side have been included, giving views of Muker with Kisdon and the Swale in the background, followed by the sight of Thwaite and the Kirkby Stephen road to the left of Kisdon and Angram, Swaledale's highest village. But be warned – this part of the walk is recommended only for well-shod walkers or in dry spells of weather, for Muker Side can be very wet.

MOTORISTS arriving in Swaledale from Wensleydale, over the wild but well-surfaced Buttertubs Pass, could park at the junction with the main Dale road just above Thwaite, picking up the route from there. This approach gives the opportunity of stopping the car at the top of the descent to Thwaite, two miles from the village, to examine the Buttertubs – pot holes by the left-hand side of the road.

Otherwise, the starting point is Muker Bridge, near which the car may be left. Leave the road immediately by walking up-hill (but down-dale) on the enclosed green track. After about 50 yards the track takes a right turn, bearing right until it points up the valley; passing a barn, it crosses a stream and steadily rises as far as the lane junction known as Three Loaning End. Level walking takes us to the gully containing Greenseat Beck; cross it on a stone bridge and take a sharp right turn into another enclosed lane going down-hill as far as a gate on the left, opposite a small barn.

Stride across a stream and join a green stony track, between walls, passing to the left of a derelict farm house and a barn. Go through a gate on to open moor; choose the wide gate below (not the narrow one to its right) and keep to the wall on your left. There is a gate in it at the bottom of the field but near it in the cross wall is a stile – go through it and across a footbridge over the beautiful Cliff Beck, cascading down to Scar Houses. The fall on the left is impressive but those below are still more so. To reach them, go through the stile in the wall on the right a few feet away from the stream, and join a single track going down to a stile by the road side. For the best view of the lowest waterfall, it is worthwhile to turn right on the road, but do not go beyond Scar Houses for the road to Thwaite is in the other direction, past the junction with the Hawes (Buttertubs Pass) road.

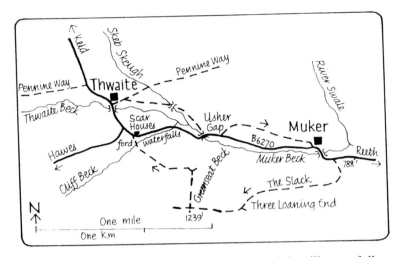

Turn right in Thwaite, going to the far end of the village to follow the direction of a Pennine Way sign to another similar one bearing additional information: "Single file – Highly cultivated land – All dogs on lead". Leave the Pennine Way here (it goes to the left) keeping straight forward on a stone trod, initially by the side of a stream, which at this point is Thwaite Beck. Cross fields by stiles and clear single paths, and pass over the beck – with the peculiar name of Skeb Skeugh – on a sheep bridge. Turn right on the other side of a stile where a notice asks you to "keep to the footpath, single file please"; the path returns to the stream side, now Muker Beck, and emerges at the road bridge.

Bear left on the road. A camping club site is in the field between road and beck. At the first farm on the left – Usher Gap – turn into the yard, bearing right to a stile, and in the field at the other side cut diagonally across to the top left-hand corner. Keep to the single track on the left of a wall and on to the west end of Muker.

Muker, River Swale, Keld and Kisdon Hill

In Swaledale's best walking area, this is the classic walk of the district and must not be missed. Muker offers much accommodation and has been popular with ramblers for generations. Here Richard and Cherry Kearton, the naturalists, went to school – as is proudly proclaimed on plaques on the walls of the school.

LEAVE the car in or near the village; take the up-hill road past the Mechanics' Institute and keep to the right of the buildings occupied by the grocer's shop. Follow the signposted route (to Gunnerside), a single file paved trod through five fields. At the last field the footbridge over the Swale will be seen on the right, but keep to the track straight forward and return to it by the waterside after going through a stile. This is the well-known Rampsholme Bridge, well constructed for pedestrians. Pools in the river below are tempting for hardy bathers. On the other side, the old coffin road to Gunnerside and the church at Grinton goes upwards to the right, but the route is to the left by the water's edge. The sheep-cropped turf, the enchanting river, the woods and gorge ahead, enclosed by hills, all combine to make a near-paradise.

Straight ahead on East Stonesdale Moor below some old workings, is Crackpot Hall – no longer occupied because of subsidence – and as one joins a double track which gradually rises on the right, the little conical Beldi Hill adds its features to the scene. The track comes to the edge of a gully, the lower end of Swinnergill with its deep gorge, waterfalls and a footbridge. Cross the bridge or the ford below it and pass old workings. Look across the valley where, on Kisdon, four distinct routes can be seen – the one near the top, beneath the crags, is the Pennine Way. Beyond Kisdon, High Seat comes into sight and below it is Keld.

Rising out of Swinnergill, take the upper of two tracks, keeping to the main track which passes below Crackpot Hall, now out of sight, and also Beldi Hill. The track then passes over the head of a scree through a gate and bears left to a point where the gorge embracing Kisdon Force can be seen – but not the Force itself, being downstream, although its position can be fixed by observation of the two river levels. Continue downhill to pass over East Gill Force on a good bridge. Turn left and enjoy looking at the three stages of the falls before passing over the Swale on a sturdy footbridge. Continue on the track up the hill; turn right at a double

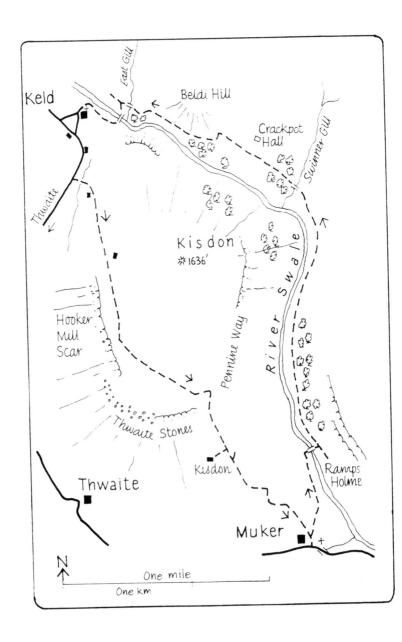

Keld

East Gill

Beldi Hill

Crackpot
Hall

Swinner Gill

Thwaite

Kisdon
*1636'

River Swale

Hooker
Mill
Scar

Pennine Way

Thwaite Stones

Thwaite

Kisdon

Ramps
Holme

Muker

N

One mile

One km

Pennine Way sign (you have been on this famous route for about 300 yards) and go along the sometimes muddy lane for 300 yards to arrive in the square at Keld. (See Walk 4 for Catrake Force.)

Turn left in the village, keeping left and turning left at a phone box, and passing the Youth Hostel away on the right – on the top road. Turning left, Kisdon is seen ahead, and the return route slopes upwards on the right of the hill. Pass Hope House Filling Station – once Cat Hole Inn – and take the next turn left off the road, by the side of a barn, on a walled road crossing the little valley and going over the beck on a stone block bridge. Initially, the main track ascends steeply past a barn, through a gate, and below a newly-renovated farm house, after which the up-hill going becomes more gradual. Pass through another gate. In good conditions the Buttertubs Pass road can be seen ahead with Lovely Seat beyond it. Away to the right is High Seat, the nab to the right of it being High Pike Hill.

Now the path is on open moor. Cliffs are in sight but just before reaching them go through two gates, leftwards, into and out of a broad intake. Pass through a grassy lane between broken walls – beware of a hole in the ground – and on to open moor again on a green track over the top of Kisdon (not quite the highest point) soon to look down on the Swale and the route of the outward journey. Pass through another gate and, rounding a bend, all of a sudden Muker comes into sight, with beautiful Swaledale stretching away eastwards. The track goes between walls and becomes somewhat wet. At this stage we are walking one field away from the Pennine Way which is on the left, soon to be joined for a brief moment, but keep going downhill into another enclosed lane to step on to a metalled road. This winds down to Muker, reaching it by way of a lane passing the old rectory and a footpath sign which reads "To Keld".

Round Kisdon Hill

To quote from a National Park notice in Muker: "Kisdon Hill is a detached outlier from the main uplands to the north and east, having been isolated by the erosive action of the river Swale, which has cut a deep gorge to the east of Keld." The hill is the hub of Upper Swaledale, inviting to be climbed or encircled. Skirted by the Pennine Way, its popularity has increased in recent years and now vies with Great Shunner Fell – also on the Pennine Way. The clear route is signposted from the road uphill from Thwaite.

PARK the car on the road side near Thwaite – there is room near the Hawes (Buttertubs Pass) road junction or in the village itself, if you intend to patronise the excellent accommodation provided in this delightful place, typical of the Dale. Walk to the bottom of the village, below the Kearton Guest House; go through a stile at a Pennine Way sign and immediately through another stile into a field on the left. Half-way along the wall on the left (about 100 yards) pass through a stile and cross a field diagonally to a stile half-way along the next wall. Thereafter go through fields on a trod, keeping to the left-hand side (right bank) of the stream called Skeb Skeugh on the valley floor – sometimes marshy – until, at the last of three barns, rise only slightly on the left-hand side of a wall. Fifty yards beyond a stile in a cross wall, there is another stile, this time in the wall on the right; go through it, turn left, cross a stream and go forward up-hill towards a barn. Pass to the right of it, continuing in the same direction to the far corner; go through a gate on to the hard road and turn right.

Now it is a road walk to Keld, but if there is much traffic then Angram and Thorns could be short circuited by the use of a field track on the right. Take the first turning to Keld where, at the lower end, is a signpost on the right "Footpath to Muker". Follow it to the first junction, where a Pennine Way sign points to the left and straight forward. Go straight on. The stony path through trees is a delight, the sight and sound of crags and rushing water adding to the pleasure. Climbing, the track becomes grassy – and often muddy for the next mile; a cairn at the top of the path indicates where to bear right, going forward on the Pennine Way, below the cliffs seen ahead. (The left-hand track is to Muker and also to Kisdon Force. If you wish to incorporate this in today's walk, see Walk 31.)

The upward path leads to a gateway in a wall, where there is a Pennine Way sign; bear left, keeping to the right of the wall bordering a wood below. Muddy conditions have no doubt been the

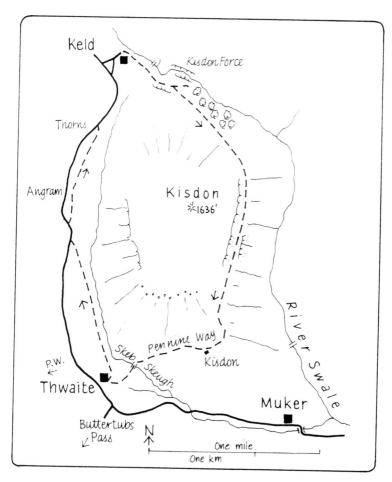

Keld

Kisdon Force

Thorns

Angram

Kisdon
✳1636'

River Swale

Pennine Way

Skeb Skeugh

Kisdon

P.W.

Thwaite

Muker

Buttertubs
Pass

N

One mile

One km

cause of deviations in the path, but it is unmistakable and when it leaves the trees it improves for a while, allowing the walker to see Swaledale below at its best. Passing through a number of stiles, you will soon see Rampsholme Bridge below and Muker to the right of it.

Just beyond an old farm building, another Pennine Way sign indicates a right turn, up-hill, into a lane to Kisdon Farm where a signpost shows still another right turn, along the bottom of a steep grass field, with a wall on the left. Turn left at the next sign, soon to bear right as indicated. Thwaite is now seen below. The wayfarer is amply guided to the beck on a double track across fields, arriving at the trod between Thwaite and Muker. Turn right, where you are asked to walk in single file on the trod back to the village.

The Waterfalls of Keld

The finest falls of Swaledale are all within a mile of Keld. They indicate the presence of a resistant band of limestone outcropping on the river bed. Wain Wath Force, Catrake Force and Kisdon Force are on the main river. East Gill Force is the lower end of the side stream, seen from the footbridge below the village. It is so close to Kisdon Force, as the crow flies, as to present difficulty to the cartographer; many people must have seen the side falls thinking they were looking at the major ones, which is a pity, for Kisdon Force is the most impressive of them all. For this reason a chapter is being devoted to a tour of the waterfalls. It must be pointed out however, that Wain Wath Force is seen on Walk 33, East Gill Force on Walk 29 and, perhaps, 32; Kisdon Force could be visited by an extension of Walk 30; and Catrake Force is at Keld's back door. Undoubtedly the best time is after rain. There is limited parking in the village but no difficulty should be experienced at quiet times of the year in leaving the car in the "square" at the lower end.

GO through the gap at the left of the square into a farm yard at the top of a cliff, at the edge of which Catrake Force is visible through the trees. A stepped path goes down to the falls which come over a ledge on a broad front. Returning to the square, cross the road to signpost "Footpath to Muker", observing, as you go, the lovely setting of this typical Swaledale village, which offers accommodation – including a Youth Hostel on the top road – for the delight of the holiday-maker. Follow the lane to the double Pennine Way signpost where the forward (upward) path is to be followed, through the trees and above the rushing Swale. At a cairn at the top, the Pennine Way track goes off to the right, but keep straight on along a stony path by the side of a wall. Going downhill towards Muker, look for a constructed gap in the wall (not merely broken down) through which a clear track turns back through a field to the cliff edge. The water can be seen in the gorge below; join a path (often muddy) sloping through the trees to Kisdon Force. The water bounds over a small upper fall into a beautiful pool and on to the lower fall – a really magnificent torrent dashing into a gorge and another pool. High limestone cliffs, trees, and clean bare rocks complete the picture. Perhaps some of its charm is its comparative inaccessibility – although, once the route is known, there is not much difficulty in reaching the falls.

Return now to the two-way Pennine Way sign and descend to the footbridge on the right for East Gill Force – three lovely stages of the final moments of the Gill before it joins the Swale. If Wain Wath

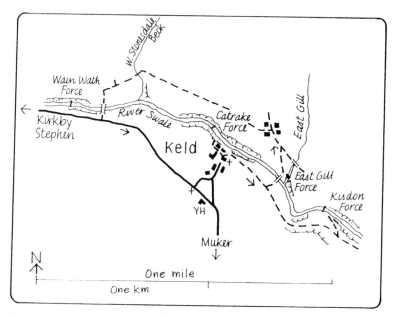

One mile

One km

Force is not to be included in today's itinerary, all that remains is to return to Keld to complete a concentrated one-and-a-half miles of beauty. If the full circuit is intended, head away from East Gill on the Pennine Way as far as the farm and leave the tarmac farmyard on the farm road, by the side of the house. Soon you should hear the sound of Catrake Force down on the left, and perhaps catch a glimpse of its white water. The farm road descends to West Stonesdale Beck and ascends to the road coming down from the hamlet of the same name. Turn left and go down the steep hill to Park Bridge, from which the prospect of Wain Wath Force pleases the eye. The main falls are the furthest away, tumbling below the high cliffs of Cotterby Scar, coming down to the lower falls and a strid-like race before reaching the bridge.

After completing such explorations as appeal to the visitor, walk up to the road junction and turn left. Half a mile of road walking brings one back to the turn down to Keld, surely with a feeling that rarely could one see so much beauty within the compass of a three-and-a-half-mile walk.

West Stonedale and Tan Hill

England's highest inn, at 1,732 feet, owes its existence to coal, which was mined in the area in the thirteenth century. The last pit to be worked closed down about 1932. The only signs now are old buildings and shafts scattered over the boggy moorland. More facts are given by Marie Hartley and Joan Ingilby in their book The Yorkshire Dales.

THE chosen start of today's walk is on the narrow road two miles north of Park Bridge, steep in its early stages but offering good wayside parking at Stonesdale Bridge and also a central position – useful for anyone wanting to halve the journey. Alternatively, Keld could be the starting point, but this might present car parking difficulties. There would also be an additional three-quarters of a mile to walk in joining and returning from the route at East Gill Force by taking the path out of the lower end of the village, sign-posted to Muker, and turning down-hill at the two-way Pennine Way sign.

From Stonesdale Bridge walk up the road for a little more than half a mile; where the road takes a sharp right-hand turn (a sheep fold is straight ahead), bear left along a tractor trail towards a bridge over the stream and another fold, joining a right of way at the bridge. Do not cross but go up-stream for 500 yards until you come to a side stream – a turf buttress, surmounted by a boulder, is on the other side. Cross the side beck and turn right, keeping to sheep tracks alongside, to rejoin the road on the right of a conical top, no doubt an old coal spoil heap. Although never far from the road, this last stretch of West Stonesdale gives the impression of eternal solitude.

Turn left, soon to reach the road junction near Tan Hill Inn, to the north of which the Pennine Way goes over flat moorland – Stainmore – to Teesdale and the fells beyond. From the inn, return by the Pennine Way on a wide coal track immediately opposite. Away to the right, more than four miles distant, is Nine Standards Rigg; on a clear day, observe the stickleback end of it – the Nine Standards themselves. Ahead are Lovely Seat, Great Shunner Fell, Hugh Seat and High Seat (from left to right).

Keep to the Pennine Way almost to Keld; it leaves the main track by bearing right to two cairns, becomes a single track by the side of a gully and passes through or skirts some marshy ground. Cross Lad Gill to a cairn above Stonesbridge and keep roughly parallel with Stonesdale Beck, passing two barns together and then

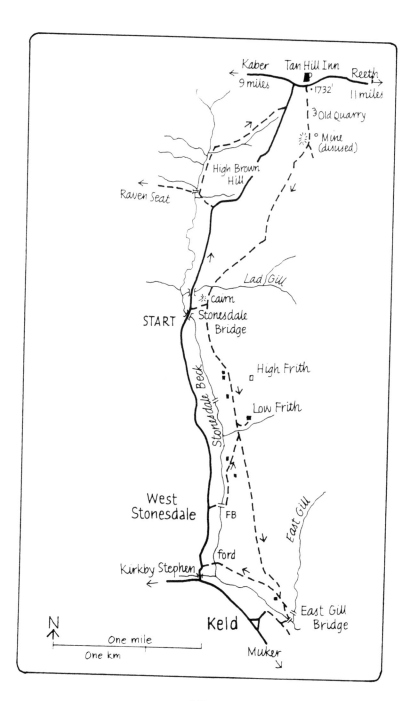

Kaber
9 miles

Tan Hill Inn

Reeth
11 miles

·1732'

³ Old Quarry

° Mine
(disused)

High Brown
Hill

Raven Seat

Lad Gill

cairn
Stonesdale
Bridge

START

High Frith

Low Frith

Stonesdale Beck

West
Stonesdale

FB

East Gill

ford

Kirkby Stephen

Keld

East Gill
Bridge

Muker

N

One mile
One km

a single barn. Make towards a gate leading to Low Frith Farm, but leave the farm track below the gate and go through a smaller one below it. Soon almost all of the rest of the Pennine Way to be walked today can be seen snaking along the hill side. Pass the hamlet of West Stonesdale on the other side of the valley; Keld then comes into sight, Kisdon rising behind and to the left of it and the tree-clad valley of the Swale further to the left. Every prospect pleases.

The track swiftly descends to a tarmac farmyard, from which the return journey is through the gate on the right on to a good stone farm road, but it is worth going on down the hill for a look at the three stages of East Gill Force. From here, those going to Keld cross the wooden bridge over the main river, bearing right up the lane away from the double Pennine Way signpost.

For the return to Stonesdale Bridge, retrace steps to the tarred farmyard and leave it by the gate to the right of the house. The farm road passes above Catrake Force which can be heard and glimpsed through trees on the left – up the valley is Cotterby Scar. Cross Stonesdale Beck, turn right on reaching the tarmac road and in less than half a mile you come to the tiny hamlet of West Stonesdale, from which there is a track on the right down to a footbridge. Cross it and continue upstream through marshy ground, over two stiles to cross a flat field on the valley floor. Make for the second of two barns adjoining the field and go through a little gate above the building. Take an upward track to the left, sloping towards the wall above, until about a hundred yards before reaching the trees by the side of a gully, go over a step stile. Continuing upwards, the undoubted track of the Pennine Way is rejoined, where soon the gate in the wall below Low Frith will be recognised. Now for a mile go back along the Pennine Way as far as the cairn above Stonesdale Bridge. The track to the left leads to the car.

Wain Wath Force and Whitsundale

Swaledale is noted for its waterfalls and gorges, and this walk takes a sample of each. Half a mile above Keld, park the car fairly near the road junction to Tan Hill and West Stonesdale. Walk down this narrow road to Park Bridge for a glorious view of Wain Wath Force, below Cotterby Scar, and lower falls of the rushing Swale.

START walking up the very steep hill, but leave the road left at the first right-hand bend where a stile leads to a track above the trees and cliffs until, on reaching beech trees, Low Bridge will be seen below. (People wishing to walk only a mile and back from here could find parking space by the road side near this bridge.) The top path forks: keep to the right to join the stone track coming up from Low Bridge. Pass one farm; immediately before the second one, Smithy Holme, take a single path on the right, skirting boggy ground. Keep roughly parallel to Whitsundale Beck, now on the left, and pass below a sheep intake on a double track. From here, on a clear day, the cairn on top of Great Shunner Fell can be seen away back on the left.

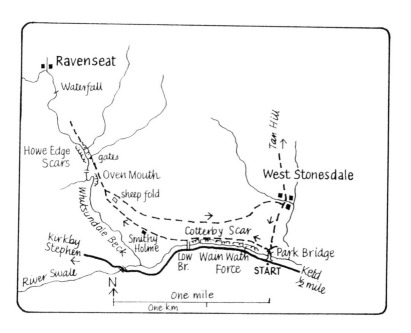

105

The double track leads to a wall at Oven Mouth, where steep crags and a sharp cleft give a fine view of the beck below. Further on, after passing through a gate and another one immediately on the left, there is a great sight of the gorge at Howe Edge Scars. A waterfall tumbles steeply through the trees to join Whitsundale Beck – a beautiful picture, particularly in autumn when the trees are a blaze of colour. This is the ultimate point of the walk, although some may wish to go further to visit a fine waterfall this side of Raven Seat and return on the same track.

Retracing one's steps, this time take the path above the large intake, from which find a single track contouring round the hill, at first towards Smithy Holme, then bearing left and keeping parallel to a wall about 300 yards away to the right. Passing under some power lines, the single track heads towards a barn where another barn is in sight. Keep to the left of both; from the end of the wall a path descends, on the edge of a gulley, to the hamlet of West Stonesdale. Pass through a gate on to the road by the side of telephone and post boxes, and turn right. Now there is a walk of less than a quarter of a mile on the road. Look over the wall on the left for views of West Stonesdale, Swaledale, and Kisdon (1,636 feet; making a fine background to a delectable scene. Go down the steep hill to Park Bridge again for a final sight of the falls.

Nine Standards Rigg

The head of Swaledale is often regarded as being the National Park boundary on the narrow road from Keld to Kirkby Stephen – although, strictly, the name of the top four miles is Birkdale. The Swale itself is formed at the confluence of Birkdale Beck and Great Sleddale Beck, both seen on the left when motoring from Keld to Kirkby Stephen. The streams are fed from the amphitheatre, seen on the left also, of Great Shunner Fell, Hugh Seat and High Seat – a wild, hagg-ridden (peat haggs) area.

THIS journey is on the ridge to the north of the road with two objects in mind; first to see as far north and north-west as possible from the boundary of the area covered by this volume; secondly to visit the curious Nine Standards, a point of call on two long distance walks – the Mallerstang Marathon and A Coast to Coast Walk. A. Wainwright, in his book on the latter walk, has the following to say: "There are many theories about the origin of the group of cairns long known as the Nine Standards, as is usually the case when the truth is not known. Certainly they are very old, appearing on 18th century maps and giving their name to the hill they adorn. They have multiplied slowly, visitors in more recent times having added a few more. They occupy a commanding position over-looking the Eden Valley, thus giving rise to the legend that they were built to give the marauding Scots the impression that an English army was encamped here. More likely they were boundary cairns (the county boundary formerly passed through them) or beacons. Harder to believe is the theory that the builders were local lads with nothing better to do to pass their time. Whatever their purpose, they were meant to endure, having suffered little from the storms of centuries."

At the top of the motor road, once the North Yorkshire/Cumbria border, is a National Park sign beside a car park. Four hundred yards into Cumbria, the terrain changes from peat to smooth grass. Park here and take the double trail to the north, on the edge of the grassy area. Limestone scars are ahead, on the side of Tailbridge Hill. Pass to the left of a mine shaft, a succession of potholes similar to the Buttertubs (Tailbridge Pots), and a small tarn. The track bends to the right towards a wall and Dukerdale, steep-sided at the top but U-shaped down below. Keeping to the right of the wall, cross the stream on stones; make for the top corner of the wall on a single path.

Rounding the wall, note two cairns on the skyline. The one on

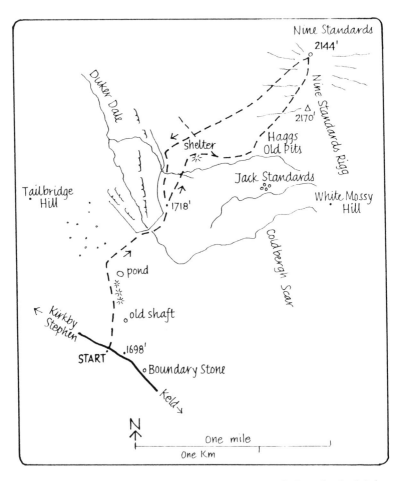

the right is at the edge of a group known as Jack Standards. Make for the left hand one, much lower – it is actually a shelter. A raised path crosses through bog; approaching a cleft, keep well up to avoid marsh; cross two small ravines about 50 yards above the confluence of streams; ascend the hill on a distinct track; pass the shelter; and join the path returning to the stream just crossed, clearly seen up-hill. Leaving the right of way, bear left at old coal spoil heaps, dodging through peat haggs on tufts in wet ground.

Once across the haggs, go up-hill leftwards; at the brow of the hill the triangulation pillar (2,170 feet) should be in sight. Although this is slightly higher than the Nine Standards (2,144 feet), the view is no better, so make for the light-coloured nab to the left; avoid some deep haggs by keeping to the left. Soon you will reach a pillar of stones on top of the Rigg – a guide to the Nine Standards which are just beyond, varying in shape and from six to thirteen feet high. Kirkby Stephen should be seen below, and across the lovely Eden valley, Little Fell, Mickle Fell and Cross Fell (in good weather) – the highest in all the Pennines. If clear, the Lakeland Fells should be visible in the west; nearer, to the south-west, beyond Wild Boar Fell, are the Howgill Fells.

To return, walk towards the Howgills on a projection of the line of the Nine Standards, at first on good short grass and moss but later through rough peat. At the edge of the Rigg, make for the cairn on Railbridge Hill, picking the best route through boggy ground; keep the shelter in sight, passing to the left of it, and on reaching the wall above Dukerdale, turn left on a track now the right of way. Cross the stream and, unless you wish to extend the walk to include Tailbridge Hill (for good going and another fine view but carrying no right of way), bear left 400 yards beyond the stream, this time keeping to the left of the limestone pavement. The Mallerstang hills are now ahead, the first being High Pike Hill, rising above the point of departure.